JOSEPH CARDINAL RATZINGER

THE MEANING OF CHRISTIAN BROTHERHOOD

JOSEPH CARDINAL RATZINGER

THE MEANING OF CHRISTIAN BROTHERHOOD

IGNATIUS PRESS   SAN FRANCISCO

Title of the German original:
Die christliche Brüderlichkeit
© 1960 Kösel-Verlag KG, Munich

First English edition © 1966, Sheed and Ward, New York
Published with ecclesiastical approval

Cover art: *Supper at Emmaus*, by Rembrandt
Paris, Louvre
Used with permission: SCALA/Art Resource, New York

Cover design by Marcia Ryan

Second English edition 1993
Ignatius Press, San Francisco
ISBN 0–89870–446–4
Library of Congress catalogue number 92–75064
Printed in the United States of America

To Professor Albert Lang
on his Seventieth Birthday

Contents

Foreword, by Scott Hahn   ix

Preface   xvii

PART ONE
A HISTORICAL ANALYSIS

The Idea of Brotherhood before and outside
  Christianity   5
    1. *"Brother" in Ancient Greece*   (5)
    2. *The Idea of Brotherhood in the Old
       Testament*   (6)
    3. *The Development in Hellenism*   (12)
    4. *The Enlightenment and Marxism*   (14)

The Development of the Idea of Brotherhood in
  Early Christianity   21
    1. *"Brother" in the Words of Christ*   (21)
    2. *The Development within the New Testament,
       Especially in Paul*   (30)
    3. *The Idea of Brotherhood in the Fathers*   (37)

PART TWO
AN ATTEMPT AT SYNTHESIS

The Basis of Christian Brotherhood: Faith   45
The Removal of Barriers within the Brotherhood of
  Christians   57
The Limits of the Brotherly Community   65
True Universalism   75

Postscript   85
Abbreviations   93

Foreword

I was once a staunch Protestant with strong anti-Catholic convictions—until I began reading myself into a crisis of faith. As a result, I resigned as pastor of my Presbyterian congregation and gave up a position as dean and instructor at a Protestant seminary. But I could not stop reading.

One day while rummaging through a shelf of theology books in a used bookstore, I picked up *Introduction to Christianity* by somebody named Joseph Ratzinger. Quite honestly, I never heard of him before. (My evangelical seminary professors paid scant attention to Catholic theologians and then only to the more maverick figures like Hans Küng and Edward Schillebeeckx. Back then I preferred it that way.) I noticed the publisher was Seabury, which markets mostly Protestant titles (Ignatius Press now carries the book), and it was translated from the German; so I figured Ratzinger was probably Lutheran or Reformed. It never occurred to me that he might be Catholic.

Whatever his denomination, I knew after reading the first few chapters that Ratzinger wrote clearly about some of the most profound but neglected truths of Christianity: the Trinity, our solidarity in Christ's divine sonship, the ecclesial form of faith, the relational meaning of "person" as a being-for-others, etc. More to the point, Ratzinger clearly grasped many things that I had only recently come to discover through long hard study. Here I had found a reliable guide.

At the time, I was out of the ministry and teaching theology at my alma mater, Grove City College. I often lunched with Dr. Andrew Hoffecker, my good friend and favorite college professor. He knew me to be a voracious reader. So over lunch he would let me share some of my recent discoveries. I seized the opportunities, fearing only that he might pick up on how Catholic-sounding more and more of my findings were—a fact I tried to hide from myself.

One day I brought *Introduction to Christianity* to lunch and read some sections to Andy. We started to discuss it. "Andy, don't you think he overturns the shallow individualism of modern theologians who confuse the God of faith with the God of philosophers? I mean, he shows how faith comes to us through the Church so believers share solidarity as members of God's family through Christ's divine sonship! Isn't that what 'covenant' really means?"

"Wow, Scott, it really sounds like he's hit upon some of your 'novel' finds. What's that author's name again?"

"Joseph Ratzinger."

"Never heard of him."

"Neither have I. He's German, but I don't know if he's Lutheran or Reformed."

A few days later I walked into Andy's office for lunch. He gave me a rather suspicious look and then handed me a copy of *Time* magazine. "Turn to the Religion Section."

So I did just that. There was a picture of a silver-haired man wearing the red hat of a Catholic cardinal. Underneath, the caption identified him as "Cardinal Ratzinger, the New Inquisitor".

"What did you say that author's name was?"

I felt my throat constrict. "It may have been Ratzinger. Yeah, that's right, Joseph Ratzinger—but not Cardinal Ratzinger. This guy's a high-ranking Vatican official in the Roman Church. It can't be the same Ratzinger."

"Check and see."

Later I went back to my office to check. Just as I feared, the two were one and the same. I never did get around to telling Andy, and fortunately he never asked.

So, Joseph Cardinal Ratzinger, a man *Time* described as "ultraconservative" and "reactionary" was now the Prefect of the Congregation for the Doctrine of the Faith. I put his book aside.

Within a matter of days, I ran across Ratzinger's name in two other titles that I picked up in another used bookstore. The first book, *Faith: Conversations with Contemporary Theologians,* was edited by Teofilo Cabestrero, a Spanish priest-journalist on assignment in Paraguay. A compilation of interviews with some of the most influential figures in contemporary theology, it was published by Orbis Books, which I knew to be the main North American purveyor of Liberation Theology. The title page listed controversial names like Hans Küng, Edward Schillebeeckx, Karl Rahner, Gustavo Gutierrez, Juan Luis Segundo—and Joseph Ratzinger?

What was Joseph Ratzinger's name doing on that list? After all, there were no other "ultraconservative" types featured, much less the Grand Inquisitor himself! Then I noticed that the book was published in 1980, shortly before Ratzinger was appointed Prefect. I became curious. How would the book portray Ratzinger before his rise to inquisitorial power?

Here are the words of Cabestrero to introduce Ratzinger:

They say that Joseph Ratzinger's reputation as a theologian has risen a great deal in this postconciliar period
because of his moderation. For that very reason, they
say, Ratzinger is one of the theologians most trusted
by even the most centrist bishops in CELAM (Episcopal
Council of Latin America). They also say that his 'balance'
earned him his rapid rise to the archbishopric of Munich
and to the cardinalate—very significant promotions at
the end of the papacy of Paul VI. I know that his name
has become well known in the last few years. I know
about the spreading influence of his writings and the
expansion of his teaching. But I don't know whether,
in all the talk about his moderation, the truth has been
clearly spoken. . . . I know only that his answers in
our conversation, without being exactly outspoken,
seemed to me of a tone that I would not dare to describe
as 'moderate', because of its realism and openness. Alert
in mind and word, this man shows a great mastery of
current philosophy and of history, and he knows today's
problems well. I did notice an extreme moderation in
his voice, in his gestures, in his face, and in his own
manner, so much so that I could not avoid the contrasting
image of Rahner. Certainly Ratzinger did not seem to
me to be German, because even the harsh German language was soft on his lips (147–48).

Ultraconservative Inquisitor, *Time* magazine? Ratzinger
was back on my "safe" list.

The second title I found that day was the original
English edition of the book you now hold in your
hands.[1] I devoured it in an evening. Since then I have

---

[1] Published in 1966 by Sheed and Ward, *The Open Circle: The
Meaning of Christian Brotherhood* was a somewhat ambiguous render-
ing of the 1960 German title, *Die christliche Brüderlichkeit:* the shorter
title of the present edition is preferred.

re-read it many times. I find it to be invaluable for gaining greater understanding in three important areas: Ratzinger's theology, the message of Scripture, and the significance of the Catholic Church.

First, this book has a foundational place in Ratzinger's own theological development. In the beginning of his scholarly career, Ratzinger devoted himself almost exclusively to patristic and medieval studies, specifically St. Augustine's ecclesiology[2] and St. Bonaventure's theology of history.[3] This book thus stands out as the first widely circulated essay addressing a doctrinal topic from Ratzinger's own personal viewpoint.[4] As such it represents his first major theological expression. Indeed, in later works, Ratzinger continually returns to many of the basic themes and concerns first treated in this book (e.g., covenant, salvation history, communion, divine sonship, solidarity, ecumenism, mission, the Church's unity and universality).

Second, in treating Christian brotherhood from the perspective of salvation history, the book opens up the meaning of both Old and New Testaments in a most

[2] Joseph Ratzinger, *Volk und Haus Gottes in Augustine Lehre von der Kirche* (Munich 1954). This work deserves to be translated and published for a wider readership; *Te rogamus audi nos.*

[3] Ratzinger, *Die Geschichtstheologie des heiligen Bonaventura* (Munich 1959); English edition: *The Theology of History in St. Bonaventure* (Chicago: Franciscan Herald Press, 1989).

[4] Aidan Nichols, *The Theology of Joseph Ratzinger: An Introductory Study* (Edinburgh: T. & T. Clark, 1988), 66. Nichols describes it as "Ratzinger's first widely disseminated essay treating of a doctrinal topic *in propria persona,* rather than by way of the exposition of some earlier father or doctor. . . . Ratzinger's treatment is both more original, and more thoughtful, than one might suppose."

essential area that has long been neglected.[5] Ratzinger
shows how brotherhood was originally based on the
fatherhood of God in creation, as well as on our common
descent from Adam and Noah. Mankind was thus created to form one worldwide *familia Dei*. The covenant
of brotherhood in God's family was then utterly broken
by sin in successive stages: at the fall, the flood and
the Tower of Babel. When God graciously made a covenant with Abraham, a new and different kind of brotherhood was formed on the basis of divine election. The
Israelites as the children of Abraham became God's special covenant family. As such they were called to holiness
so that the other nations might eventually be led back
into brotherhood. This plan constituted a universal mission that Israel seldom understood, much less obeyed.
Accordingly, Christ made a new covenant in himself—
as the only Son of God—so that through baptism we
might share his divine sonship by faith. "Thus the ideas
of fatherhood-sonship-brotherhood acquire a completely new ring, the ring of reality" (49). "To become
a Christian means to become incorporated in the Son,
in Christ, so that we become 'sons in the Son'" (53).
Ratzinger has captured the very heart and soul of
Scripture.

Third, Ratzinger explains how a proper sense of
Christian brotherhood leads to a better understanding
of the Catholic Church, showing that the former is
only fulfilled in the latter. He does this in the second

[5] The last major book in English to concentrate on the biblical
idea of brotherhood is A.S. Peake, *Brotherhood in the Old Testament*
(New York: George H. Doran Company, 1923). Besides being somewhat dated, Peake's study does not even consider brotherhood in
the New Testament.

part of the book, "An Attempt at Synthesis", where
he applies the historical analysis of the first part to difficult issues regarding the Church's unity and universality.
Let me highlight two of his considerations.

First, having established the distinctively Christian
sense of brotherhood (vis-à-vis Judaism, Hellenism,
Stoicism, the Enlightenment, and Marxism), Ratzinger
shows how fraternal solidarity can only be perfected
through God's fatherhood and Christ's divine sonship
by means of the Eucharist.

> The brotherly community of the Christians consists of
> those, and only those, who come with at least a cer-
> tain regularity to share in the eucharistic celebration. . . .
> For only on this view can we hope, with any justifi-
> cation, for an actual realization of a conscious brotherly
> community (73).

Ratzinger insists this does not mean we can write off
those who are outside the brotherhood. "On the contrary, it means that we must rid ourselves of a dangerous
illusion that can easily prevent us from recognizing the
true measure of our responsibility toward those whose
brothers we could be, but unfortunately all too little
are" (73–74).

Second, Ratzinger explains how God's gift of fraternal
communion also implies a human imperative: the removal of barriers within the brotherhood of Christians.
These barriers may come from outside the Church; so
he refers to "the overcoming of nationalism" (59). Or
they may arise from within the Church, where an "ethos
of hierarchic differences" is challenged by Jesus' own
words: "And call no man your father on earth, for
you have one Father, who is in heaven. Neither be

called masters, for you have one master, the Christ. He who is greatest among you shall be your servant" (Mt 23:9–11). Ratzinger explains: "If we take the preceding verses (1–8) as well, it is clear the false hierarchism and dignity of office cultivated by the Jews is contrasted with the undifferentiated brotherliness of Christians" (59–60). Instead of undermining the Catholic priesthood, Jesus's words actually reveal its true fraternal character: "We might add that, as 'father', he still remains a 'brother'; his fatherly office is a form of brotherly service, and nothing else" (62).

From these and other similar considerations, Ratzinger reaches a rather striking conclusion: "The dogmatic position is that the objective presentation of the vicarious saving act of Jesus Christ can be performed by the one true Church only, that is (according to Catholic belief) the Catholic Church which is gathered around the successor of Peter" (89).

Hard-hitting words, to be sure—especially when they first fell upon my Protestant ears. But they are no less loving, if indeed they are true. After a long-fought battle, with much study and prayer, I concluded that they were. I was received into the Eucharistic brotherhood of God's family, the Catholic Church, Easter Vigil 1986. Thanks be to God—and to my dear brother, Joseph Cardinal Ratzinger.

SCOTT HAHN
January 25, 1993
Feast of the Conversion of St. Paul

Preface

The following essay was first read to the Theological Congress of the Austrian Institute for Pastoral Work in Vienna at Easter 1958 and subsequently published in *Seelsorger,* 1958, 387–429. This accounts for its historical and factual limitations, as it is intended to be more an invitation to discussion than a definitive treatment of the subject. That such discussion is to be wished for among a wider circle than hitherto is the justification for its publication in a virtually unaltered form.

JOSEPH RATZINGER

Bonn

ONE

A HISTORICAL ANALYSIS

"You have but one teacher, and you are all brothers" (Mt 23:8). These words of Christ define the relationship between Christians as a relationship of brothers, and thus contrast with the natural brotherhood of blood relationship a new brotherhood of the spirit. So the Christian ethos is, or should be, an ethos of brotherliness. In order to grasp the significance, the extent, and the limits of this new brotherhood, we propose examining the various conceptions of brotherhood which are to be found within early Christianity and those which developed from it later. In this way we shall hope to discover what is specifically Christian about it.

The Idea of Brotherhood before and outside Christianity

"Brother" in Ancient Greece

Brotherhood is, as we have said, primarily a phenomenon of blood relationship; but the metaphorical use of the term is very old, even if there is not much documentary evidence for it. In Plato we find the description of one's fellow citizen as a brother[1] (*Menexenos,* 239 a): "We and our fellow citizens are all brothers born of one another." Xenophon calls a friend a "brother" (*Anabasis,* II, 2, 25; 38). In the former case, brotherhood is based on the extended blood relationship of a nation; in the latter, on what we may, with Goethe, call an "elective affinity". In both cases brotherhood implies a frontier. In Plato, if the community of the state bestows brotherhood, then the foreigner, the *barbaros,* is regarded as a nonbrother; Xenophon's brotherhood of friends not only unites friends, but also divides off those who are not friends. All unions involve the separating of those who are united together from others. Although neither Plato nor Xenophon specifically refers to it, the basic problem of every brotherhood ethos arises here. If, for example, the people united in one *polis* form a

---

[1] Quoted in H. von Soden's article on *adelphos* (brother) in *TWNT,* I, 146, 3f.; and in K. H. Schelkle's article on *bruder* (brother) in *RAC,* II, 631.

5

brotherhood, the ethos within that *polis* will necessarily differ from the attitude toward those outside it, who are not brothers: ethical responsibility is different within the "extended family" than outside it. In other words, this broadened concept of brotherhood inevitably creates two different kinds of ethos. This is a basic human tension, seen in its most extreme form in the idea of brotherhood, and, as we shall see, in Christianity itself.

The Idea of Brotherhood in the Old Testament

Whereas we find only scattered references in the Greek world, in Old Testament Israel "brother" was a fixed term of address. Here one's coreligionist generally had the title *ah* (brother).[2] It was the common religion which seemed to be in the forefront of their consciousness here: when merely a compatriot was meant, the word *re'a* (neighbor) was used;[3] in rabbinical writings the two were sometimes even carefully distinguished. This, it is true, was a later development, for originally the religious community and the national community were one. There is undoubtedly a genuine similarity between the structures of the Greek *polis* and of the theocracy of the Old Testament. In both cases the political unit was taken also as the religious one, and the religious community was the same as the political: the Church was the state, and vice versa.[4] Thus the problem which we have already noted recurs here: the presence of two zones of ethical being, clearly formulated in the two

[2] Examples in Von Soden, 145; and Schelkle, *RAC,* II, 635f.
[3] Von Soden, 145.
[4] See J. Ratzinger, *Volk und Haus Gottes in Augustins Lehre von der Kirche* (Munich, 1954), 255–76.

opposed terms *am* and *gojim* ("people" and "Gentiles").
The biblical question "Who is my neighbor?" is concerned with this very problem.

The particular quality of Old Testament religion col-
ored the problem in a special way. For the individual,
a brother was one who belonged with him in the unity
not of just any people, but of the unique Chosen People
of God. That meant that brotherhood did not depend
merely on common racial descent, but on common election by God. It was a brotherhood in which it was
not the common mother (the *polis?*)[5] which mattered,
but the common Father, that is, the universal God,
Yahweh. Here we come upon the special charge that
the Israelite idea of brotherhood carried. It implied
brotherhood with a common Father, God, who was
not, however, merely the God of Israel, but the one
and only God. And so he was the Father not of Israel
alone, but of all.[6] This was the strange paradox of Old
Testament religion as a whole: that Israel's national god
was the universal God, that, indeed, Israel did not have
a national god at all, but a supranational one. This almost
implies an impossibility of forming a unity within the
brotherhood of one's own nation, or else it could—
through a false development—lead to a kind of internal
ossification. It all depends on how the connection is
seen between this non-national, universal God, on the

[5] Concerning the maternal character of the *polis,* see ibid., esp.
274. We see it as an idea common to the ancient world in such
texts as Gal 4:26: "Jerusalem . . . is our mother."

[6] See texts like Ex 4:22, Ps 82, and especially Dt 32:8. For the
latter, see Quell, *TWNT,* V, 965. For the whole problem, see Martin
Buber's *An der Wende: Reden uber das Judentum,* Cologne-Olten 1952;
J. Daniélou, *The Lord of History* (London, 1958), 59–71, with further
examples.

one hand, and the people who nevertheless worship him as *their* God, on the other. In the Old Testament it is clear that this connection was made not by Israel, but by God, that he chose Israel for no merits of its own, but by a free decision of his grace, and that he could therefore freely reject it (for which all its subsequent transgressions would provide more than sufficient justification).[7] Thus God had a special paternity toward Israel: whereas he was the Father of all the peoples of the world through creation, he was beyond that the Father of Israel through election.[8] But this special situation was the free disposition of God, and it could therefore be altered at any time. This brought an element of uncertainty into any tendency to separate off the brotherly community of Israel too rigidly. In fact, the prophets always tried to arouse this sense of the potential openness of the Israelite religion both in their prophecies of doom to Israel and in their prophecies of salvation. These always opened onto a universal horizon.

The other possibility implicit in the basic paradox of the Jewish idea of God was made explicit in later Judaism. As the process of rationalizing the whole conception of religion developed, a free and uncaused elective decision by God no longer seemed appropriate. Thus the idea was born that, though God had offered all the peoples of the world the Torah, only Israel had accepted it and had thus become the unique People of

---

[7] This idea of possible rejection is a basic theme of all the prophets down to John the Baptist (Mt 3:9). The idea of free election is particularly well expressed in Ezek 6:1–14.

[8] See footnote 1 above.

God.[9] In the last analysis, this means that it was not God who chose Israel, but Israel who was the only people to take God as its god. By this time, however, the idea that the God of the people was in fact the God of the universe no longer had the effect of "opening up" Israel; on the contrary, it led to an even stricter sealing-off from those who had voluntarily renounced the special paternity of God and, therefore, the brotherly love of his children. We are here at the threshold which separates the Old Testament as *praeparatio evangelica* from Judaism as the "synagogue". In both cases, however, we can see the new tension (new, that is, compared to Greek ideas) created by the ethos of brotherhood through subordination to the paternity of the universal God.

This tension comes into the Old Testament concept of brotherhood due to its idea of God, which has a parallel with its idea of man. Over against the "closed" community which comes from Abraham, Isaac, and Jacob, there stands the universal horizon of biblical history which, at root, is not simply a history of Israel, but sets the history of Israel within the universal history of the one humanity. All men, Israelites and Gentiles, ultimately constituted a single humanity because of their single human source and the single creative act of God.

This unity of all men is shown twice: once in the creation account, in which God formed "Adam" (that is, mankind), the root of all the other men to come, in his likeness; and a second time in Noah, with whom

[9] See SB-*KNT*, III, 2nd ed., (Munich, 1954) 139ff.; G. F. Moore, *Judaism*, I (Cambridge, 1927), 274ff. The corresponding Haggadic idea is found in (among other sources) Philo, Baruch's Apocalypse, 4 Ezra, and the Talmud.

a new race of men is started after the catastrophe of
the first race. The genealogies of Genesis 10 endeavor
to prove in detail that the whole of historical humanity
owes its existence to God's saving covenant of grace
with Noah and can live only under the constant care
of God assured in that covenant.[10] On the other hand,
it still remains that God made a special covenant with
Abraham which separates the children of Abraham as
a special family from the great human family of the
children of Adam (or, rather, of Noah). Thus we can
see that both the unity and the duality of the ethos
have as their two starting points the image of God and
the image of man. The *unity* is attested by the uniqueness
of God and the common father of mankind, Adam or
Noah (both of whom create a religious community of
men insofar as both are accorded a lasting relationship
with God: the likeness to God in the case of Adam;
the covenant with God in the case of Noah); the *duality*
comes from the elective exclusiveness of God toward
Israel and the exclusive descent from the fathers of the
covenant, Abraham, Isaac, and Jacob.

In practical terms, this meant that direct brotherhood
applied only to those who shared one's country and
faith. The ethical responsibility an Israelite bore toward
another Israelite was different from that he bore toward
a Gentile. Thus there were two kinds of ethical relationship here: my neighbor is distinct from a man who is
far from me; my brother is distinct from my fellow
man. To the question "Who is my neighbor?" there
was a simple and clear answer: "My coreligionist and

[10] See commentaries on Genesis; e.g., B. H. Junker, *Genesis*
(Wurzburg, 1949), 36; G. von Rad, *Genesis* (London, 1961), 135ff.

compatriot." This evident and undeniable duality could never degenerate into dualism, however, as was possible in the Greek world and in the religions of the countries surrounding Israel; rather, it was held together through the unity of God and the unity of humanity, so that human responsibility went beyond the framework of the brotherly community, as is shown concretely by the Old Testament's laws concerning strangers (Ex 22:20; 23:9; Dt 14:29, and elsewhere; Lv 19:33f.; 19:10; 23:22; Nb 9:14; 15:14ff.; 35:15).[11] But in order to understand correctly the relationship between these two zones of ethics, it is important to note the dualities of brothers in the Old Testament. At important points in salvation history there appear pairs of brothers, the election or rejection of each of whom is strangely connected. These are, in particular, Cain and Abel (and Cain and Seth), Ishmael and Isaac, Esau and Jacob. That this is a theologically planned pattern seems clear, particularly as in one place we read that Abraham had a number of other sons apart from Isaac and Ishmael (Gen 25:1–6).[12] The full meaning of this "theology of two brothers", as one may call it, becomes clear only in the New Testament and the Fathers. Nevertheless we can still see here that even the partners of Israel who were expelled from the election could yet be understood in a wider sense as "brothers", that even he who was rejected remained a "brother"— especially when rejection and election are switched in such a strange way as with Esau and

[11] See also the article "Fremde" (stranger) in H. Haag, *Bibellexikon* (Einsiedeln, 1951), 495, and the appropriate section of the article *xenos* (stranger) by G. Stahlin in *TWNT*, V, 8–16.

[12] See Karl Barth's view of election, outlined briefly below in Part Two, for an understanding of this pattern.

a secret society whose mystic ethos seemed criminal to those outside.

Simultaneous with this development of new, narrowly circumscribed fraternities, there was also an exactly opposite development. Political unification had its philosophical parallel in Stoic cosmopolitanism which discovered the unity of the world and of men. Epictetus saw all men as brothers, for all came from God.[16] The ideas of the Stoa, of Seneca, Musonius, and Marcus Aurelius, followed the same direction.[17] Thus one basic ethos of brotherliness was appropriate to all men. In the Hermes mystery cult this idea of the universal paternity of God and of the brotherhood of his children—mankind—found a direct religious expression. The uninitiated were the "ignorant brothers", whom the enlightened remembered when they prayed to the Father. "Fill me with thy strength," the mystic prayed, "and then I shall enlighten with this grace those of my people who live in ignorance, my brothers, your children."[18]

The Enlightenment and Marxism

The idea of a single, all-embracing brotherhood resounded strongly in the period of eighteenth-century Enlightenment, and it is in the thought of this time

[16] E. Zeller, *Outlines of the History of Greek Philosophy* (London, 1931), 269ff.

[17] Zeller, 266ff.; 268 n. 1; 269; 271.

[18] *Corpus Hermeticum*, 1, 32, quoted in Schelkle, *RAC*, II, 634. The whole text is translated in O. Casel, *Das Gedachtnis des Herrn* (1919), 44ff.

that it found its most radical and effective form. The French Revolution proclaimed *liberté, egalité, fraternité,* and made the brotherhood of men with equal rights a political, revolutionary program. The origin of this brotherhood in the common paternity of God now moved very much into the background. It has too remote, too hypothetical a ring when Schiller sings in his "Ode to Joy": "Brothers, above the starry sky there must dwell a loving father"; the brotherhood of man seems independent of this idea. It is conceived as coming from this world, from the similar heredity and nature of all men. It involves going behind history to the nature of man that is anterior to it.[19] All differences between men come from positive action, that is, from man's willful behavior in history. They are what Kant calls something merely "statutary", whereas before and above them stands the natural equality of all. The reestablishment and the continuing respect for natural equality—the original brotherhood of *all* men—was the aim of the French Revolution. We must assist original nature to be victorious over the subsequent misdealings of history. The question whether history could really be subordinated to nature in this way was never asked.

As can be seen, the problem of the extended idea of brotherhood was here solved in a very radical way: brotherhood no longer created two separate zones of ethical behavior; on the contrary, in the name of brotherhood all barriers were removed and a unified ethos was proclaimed as binding on all men in equal measure.

---

[19] See G. Söhngen, "Vom Wesen des Christentums", *Die Einheit in der Theologie* (Munich, 1952), 288–304. He interprets the Enlightenment as a radical liberation of man from history.

This sweeping away of all divisions has something splendid about it, but it is dearly bought, for brotherhood, extended so far, becomes unrealistic and meaningless. The naïveté of Schiller's "Be embraced ye millions" has often been remarked on in this connection. In fact, a brotherliness which embraces everyone equally cannot expect to be taken seriously by anyone. This insight rather deepens the problem we have set ourselves, for it raises these questions: Must an ethos, to be realizable, perhaps contain some form of duality? Does it inevitably require a closed "inner ring" to be fully workable? We should remember here that the program of the Enlightenment did not emerge very well as realized through the French Revolution which differentiated drastically and bloodily between the inner fraternal circle of the revolutionaries and the outer circle of the nonrevolutionaries. We must also remember that liberalism, the heir of the Enlightenment ideology, also created in freemasonry its own highly differentiated inner fraternal group.

From the Enlightenment the path leads directly to the Marxist idea of fraternity. That the word "comrade" is preferred to "brother" is of secondary importance, although it does indicate a different emphasis in Marxist ideology. The idea of God as the common Father has finally disappeared, but the idea of common humanity has also lost some of its importance through the commitment to a socialist community. What most distinguishes Marxism from the thinking of the Enlightenment is the decisive return to the idea of two ethical zones, here carried through with a radicality unparallelled in history. No longer is there any idea of the equal brotherhood of all men; rather, humanity is divided into two totally antithetical groups, capital and proletariat, and their embattled dialectic constitutes history. Fate and, to some extent, his own decision put a man—as we have already suggested—on one or the other side of divided humanity. Whichever side he is on, however, man has to accept this division as given. It provides him with the law of his human behavior. He cannot treat all men as brothers, but only some; the others are enemies. If he loves one group, he is forced to side with them and fight the others. Hence Marxism involves, from the beginning, a division of the world, intended by Marx as a purely social division; now—as a result of the Russian Revolution and of world politics— Marxism has become a political division into two opposing blocs of states. However little this may correspond to Marx's original conception, it is a logical development from it. Brotherhood toward some involves enmity toward others.

This dualism, of course, is not the last word about Marxism. Rather, the present struggle of divided mankind takes place in the hope of its eschatological reunion in the condition of the classless society. But this reunion lies beyond history; it is the enduring final condition of mankind. Here we come upon an idea that is shared with the Enlightenment: for Marxism, too, the division of mankind is given historically, the fall of history away from nature, the self-alienation of man. But Marxism has a far clearer idea of the nature of this self-alienation than the Enlightenment, and above all it seeks the conquest over this historical alienation—the return to pure nature—not in a vague, emotional idea of universal brotherhood, but in the stern discipline of a hard and purposeful fight. The goal is also the unified, undifferentiated brotherhood of all men; but the way is the limited brotherhood of the socialist party, the acknowledgment of a divided humanity.[20]

So far we have outlined the most important non-Christian forms of the idea of brotherhood. It is obvious that each of the conceptions we have described has some relationship to Christianity. Some of them were even confused with Christian ideas, or regarded themselves as true Christianity; conceptions as different from each other as the Enlightenment's ethos of universal brotherhood and the closed world of the mysteries were equated with Christianity. The confusion between the brotherly love of the Enlightenment and the universal Christian love of one's neighbor, at least in some of its forms, is still more widely disseminated than one might think. On the other hand, the researches of Otto Casel in our century have given renewed cause to see Christianity, in terms of the phenomenology of religion, under the *eidos* of the mystery cult—that is, as a religious type of the mystery covenant.[21] Whether one or the other or neither is correct is obviously of central importance

[20] Apart from the basic work by G. A. Wetter, *Dialectical Materialism: A Historical and Systematic Survey of Philosophy in the Soviet Union* (London, 1958), see the instructive essay by J. Lacroix, "Der marxistische Mensch", *Dokumente* (1948), vols. 1 and 2, and K. Löwith, *Weltgeschichte und Heilsgeschehen* (Stuttgart, 1953), 38–54.

[21] A comprehensive survey of Casel's work can be found in T. Filthaut, *Die Kontroverse uber die Mysterienlehre* (Warendorf, 1947); see particularly 86–98.

for determining the idea of Christian brotherhood. On the other hand, we can also see that an understanding of the Christian idea of brotherhood is not just peripheral, but can contribute greatly to a correct typological formulation of the Christian religion.

The Development of the Idea of Brotherhood in Early Christianity

"Brother" in the Words of Christ

Before we can attempt a comprehensive factual and dogmatic definition of the Christian idea of brotherhood, it seems necessary to set out simply what is given historically in the New Testament and the Fathers.

When we examine the appropriate texts in the New Testament, the first thing we notice is that, at least in terminology, there is no one consistent idea of brotherhood that goes through them all. In the early texts the Jewish terminology is simply taken over;[1] but at the same time there starts to develop, first tentatively but ever more independently, a Christian use of the term which finally, by the latest texts of Scripture—that is, in John—is totally distinct (1 Jn 2:9, 10; 3:10, 16, 17; 5:16; 3 Jn 3, 5, 10).[2] Here we come upon the problem, explored particularly by Dutch philologists, of the spe-

---

[1] Schelkle, *RAC,* II, 636, quotes as examples of this Jewish usage Acts 2:29, 37; 7:2; 13:15, 26; 22:1, 5; 28:15, 21; James 1:9; 2:15; 4:11; Mt 5:22, 24, 47; 7:3, 4, 5; 18:15, 21, 35.

[2] As we shall see, one should probably also include here some of the Matthew texts, which may well reflect the perfected terminology of a Christian community rather than the formulations of Christ before the separation from the Jewish fraternal community.

cial language of the early Christians.[3] Here, too, we can see how the idea of "brother" was further developed in the Fathers but then became quickly less important. This linguistic process is of great interest, because in it we can see, in a particularly tangible way, how the Christian community gradually developed to become an independent church, how early Christianity grew and became firmly grounded. Let us start with Christ's use of the word "brother". Schelkle distinguishes in his utterances three chief usages. The first group of texts simply takes over the Old Testament Jewish use: "brother" meant one's *Jewish* coreligionist. All these texts are to be found in Matthew's Gospel.

> You have heard that it was said to the men of old: "You shall not kill; and whoever kills shall be liable to judgment." But I say to you that every one who is angry with his brother shall be liable to judgment; whoever insults his brother shall be liable to the council, and whoever says, "You fool!" shall be liable to the hell of fire. So if you are offering your gift at the altar, and there remember that your brother has something against you, leave your gift there before the altar and go; first be reconciled to your brother, and then come and offer your gift (5:21–24).

> Why do you see the speck that is in your brother's eye, but do not notice the log that is in your own eye? (7:3; cf. 7:4–5)

[3] See in particular the work of C. Mohrmann, especially *Die altchristliche Sondersprache in den Sermones des hl. Augustin,* I (Nijmegen, 1932). Also important is H. Janssen's *Kultur und Sprache: zur Geschichte der alten Kirche im Spiegel der Sprachentwicklung—Von Tertullian bis Cyprian* (Nijmegen, 1938). A critical discussion of the question of a special language can be found in H. Becker, *Tertullians Apologeticum: Werden und Leistung* (Munich, 1954), 335–45.

If your brother sins against you, go and tell him his
fault, between you and him alone. If he listens to you,
you have gained your brother. But if he does not listen,
take one or two others along with you, that every word
may be confirmed by the evidence of two or three wit-
nesses. If he refuses to listen to them, tell it to the church;
and if he refuses to listen even to the church, let him
be to you as a Gentile and a tax collector (18:15ff.; cf.
18:21 about how often to forgive, and 18:35: "So also
my heavenly Father will do to every one of you, if you
do not forgive your brother from your heart").

In the important text of Matthew 18:15ff., at any rate,
we must assume a strong influence from the usage of
the community,[4] and this is probably the case with the
other texts as well.[5] This means that these texts do
not give us directly the terminology of Christ, but of
the Jewish Christian community, thus representing an
already comparatively settled condition of Christian usage. However, the word "brother" in this connection
could certainly go back to Jesus himself, as is suggested
by the comparison between Matthew 18:15ff. and Luke
17:3. In this case the developed community of Saint
Matthew's Gospel, because of their new situation, would
have understood something else in the words of Jesus
than was originally directly intended—the new Christian
brotherly community, rather than the old Jewish religious and national community. This reinterpretation
was possible because of the analogy between both
groups; after Jesus, a new religious community had de-

[4] See J. Schmid, *Das Evangelium nach Matthaus*, 3rd ed. (Regensburg New Testament, 1), (1956), 271ff.
[5] Certainly this seems clear in 5:23ff. This text is understood in
the *Didache*, XIV, 2, as a rule of the community, and was probably
also understood as such when it was taken into the Greek Matthew.

veloped which resembled in structure the old Jewish religious community. Nevertheless, in this first group of texts from the mouth of Jesus we meet, not his own new message of brotherhood, but either the language of a Christian community that is already fairly developed or else words of Jesus which merely take over the language of his Jewish environment.

A second group of texts comprises those of his utterances in which he does not follow the general Jewish usage, but the special use of the word "brother" which the rabbis used to describe their pupils. To this group Schelkle ascribes the well-known words of Christ to Peter at the Last Supper: "Simon, Simon, behold, Satan demanded to have you, that he might sift you like wheat, but I have prayed for you that your faith may not fail; and when you have turned again, strengthen your brothers" (Lk 22:31). Two utterances of the risen Christ also belong in this group. One is the words, recorded by Matthew, that he addressed to the women who were the first to meet him, when he told them to "go and tell my brothers to go to Galilee, and there they will see me" (Mt 28:10). The other, found in John, opens up deeper theological perspectives, and thus transcends the rabbinical framework. Here he tells Mary Magdalene: "Go to my brothers and say to them, I am ascending to my Father and your Father, to my God and your God" (Jn 20:17b). The brotherhood of the disciples among one another and with Christ is here closely connected with the fatherhood of God and thus is raised to a quite different level than the mere teacher-pupil relationship which the rabbinical use of "brother" signified. Schelkle is right to include here too, at least formally, the important words of Jesus in Matthew 22:8, which could well be the motto of our investigation: "You are not to be called rabbi, for you have one teacher, and you are all brothers."[6] It is, however, clear that in content this sentence implies the end of rabbinism, the Christian revolution, the lessening of all worldly distinctions in the face of the encounter with the one who is truly great, truly different—Christ. Thus in these words which formally represent rabbinical usage, there breaks through the new Christian idea of brotherhood. Indeed, perhaps all the texts of this second group represent a progression toward the definitive Christian usage. Formally it is rabbinical if the master (i.e., rabbi) calls his disciples his brothers; but in order to assess the implications of this for the future, it is necessary to consider the self-awareness of this particular master and the consciousness that he had of the importance of his disciples. On the latter point in particular the Gospels leave us in no doubt; when Jesus chose twelve disciples, he chose a symbolic number whose significance was obvious for every reader of Scripture. He places himself in the position of Jacob and his twelve sons who became the twelve patriarchs of the Chosen People of Israel; in this way he showed that here a new, truer "Israel" was beginning. The twelve, who were not called apostles to start with, but only *hoi dodeka,* are marked out by their number as the spiritual patriarchs of a new, spiritual People of God.[7]

[6] Schelkle, *RAC,* II, 636. We find also the rabbinical usage in I Tim 5:1.

[7] See F. M. Braun, *Neues Licht auf die Kirche* (Einsiedeln 1946), 71; A. Fridrichsen, "Messias und Kirche", *Ein Buch von der Kirche,* ed. Aulén, Fridrichsen, Nygren et al. (Göttingen 1951), 33. See especially K. H. Rengstorf's article on *dodeka* in *TWNT,* II, 321–28.

When Jesus calls his disciples "brothers", then, it is something quite different from an ordinary rabbi speaking of his pupils. It is a decision for the future, for in these twelve the new People of God is being addressed; in them it is being designated as a people of brothers, a great new brotherhood. In other words, in the eyes of Jesus the twelve are not a group of rabbinical pupils (just as he did not regard himself as a rabbi), rather, they correspond to the people of Israel, symbolizing them at a higher level, and recapitulate the brotherhood of the old Israel which we considered before.

Let us now proceed to the third group of texts in which Jesus uses the word "brother". This time it is a typically Christian usage. Schelkle mentions here particularly Mark 3:31–35. When told that his mother and his brothers are outside, "Jesus replied, 'Who are my mother and my brothers?' And looking around on those who sat about him, he said, 'Here are my mother and my brothers! Whoever does the will of God is my brother, and sister, and mother.' " In the place of blood relationship, and surpassing it, is set spiritual relationship. For Jesus, brothers are those who are united with him in the common acceptance of the will of God.[8] The difference from the ideology of the Enlightenment and the general brotherhood of the Stoics is obvious: brotherhood is not seen naturalistically, as an original

---

[8] Similarly Jn 14:21: "He who has my commandments and keeps them, he it is who loves me; and he who loves me will be loved by my Father"; cf. 15:14ff. It is notable that John here replaces the word *adelphos* (brother) by *philos* (friend), and that the fourth Gospel uses the word *adelphos* outside the meaning of blood relationship only in two places: 20:17 and 21:23.

phenomenon of nature, but depends on a decision of the spirit, a saying "yes" to the will of God.

The second text to which Schelkle refers here is more influenced by the terminology of the community. It is Mark 10:29 where Jesus promises to him who leaves his brothers, sisters, father, mother, children, or lands for his sake and in order to preach the gospel the return of all he had left even in this life, even though there would be persecutions as well. It is surely true to say that the new and greater family that is here promised to the missionary is composed of the members of the Christian communities looked after by him. This is, in fact, the same idea as before, only more strongly influenced by the idea of an already existent Christian community. It follows that the community of will with the Father is conceived more concretely, too, as acceptance of the Christian Faith.

In the great judgment parable of Matthew 25:31–46 we find a quite different conception of the Christian idea of brotherhood. The difference is so marked that it can hardly be grouped with any of the texts we have considered hitherto.[9] The judge of the world declares to those gathered before his tribunal that the works of mercy done (or not done) for those in need were done (or not done) for himself, and he calls these people in need "the least of these my brothers" (25:40). Nothing suggests that only the faithful, only believers in the gospel of Christ, are meant here, as is the case in a similar text (Mk 9:41), but rather all people in need,

[9] Schelkle, RAC, II, 637, places it in the third group, which is justified inasmuch as it is a specifically Christian text. Within this group, however, it has a unique position.

without differentiation.[10] On the other hand, it is not permissible to conclude from the expression "the least of these my brothers" that the judge of the world is calling all men his brothers and only among them those in need. A large number of texts show that Christ sees himself generally represented in the poor and lowly especially, people who—quite apart from their ethical quality, but simply through their being lowly, and the appeal to the love of others that lies in that—make present the Master.[11] Instead of calling them "the least of [his] brothers", it would be more correct to translate: "my brothers (i.e., the least)". The *elakhistoi* are, as such, the brothers of the Lord, who has made himself the least of men.[12] Brotherhood with Christ is founded here not, as before, on the freely chosen community of will and conviction, but on the community of lowliness and suffering. This text is important because it expresses a universality which does not exist in what we have considered hitherto. If the community of the disciples is the basis of a new Israel, and thus of a new fraternal community, then we might expect that the closed brotherhood of Israel would repeat itself once more. The question "Who is my neighbor?" would then receive a different answer, but structurally it would be the same

[10] Thus Schmid, *Matthaus*, 355.

[11] This appears clearly from the frequent emphasis of the *mikroi* (lowly, humble). See Mt 10:42; 11:11; 18:6, 10. See also O. Michel's article on *mikros* in *TWNT*, IV, 650–56.

[12] Compare the idea of Jesus as the Son of Man, in which both Daniel's idea of sovereignty and Isaiah's idea of the remnant are combined. *See* J. Schmid, *Das Evangelium nach Markus,* 3rd ed. (Regensburg New Testament, 2), (1954), 160ff. See also the important Marcan text 10:41–45, and the washing of the feet, Jn 13:1–20.

as the old one. One's neighbor would now no longer be one's compatriot, one's coreligionist in an essentially national faith, but the fellow believer in the nonpolitical, spiritual faith of Christ. He who has read the judgment parable of Matthew 25 knows why the answer of Jesus is different in the parable of the Good Samaritan (Lk 10:30–37). My neighbor is the first man I meet who is in need, for, as such, he is simply a brother of the Master who is always present to me in the lowliest of men. This raises the question whether, in these texts (Mt 25:31–46 and Lk 10:30–37), which we spontaneously feel to be the most sublime, the unlimited brotherhood of the Enlightenment—at least in its purest forms, such as in Lessing's *Nathan*—is not in fact fulfilled? It is true that there is here an ultimate removal of barriers which one finds in so complete a form only in Stoicism and the Enlightenment. Nevertheless, there is in the gospel a christological element in the idea of brotherhood which creates a quite different spiritual atmosphere from the Enlightenment ideology. But even apart from this, the other texts remain which, unlike this last and open idea of brotherhood, suggest a more or less closed one. Thus the brotherhood texts which proceed from the mouth of Jesus present us with an open question. On the one hand, it is clear that all those who need help are, irrespective of any barriers, through their very plight the brothers of Jesus. On the other hand, it is also apparent that the coming community of the faithful will form a new fraternal community which will be distinct from those who do not believe. Thus we have a limited conception on one side, and a universal one on the other. It remains unresolved how they are related to each other.

The Development within the New Testament, Especially in Paul

If we turn now to the development of the idea of brotherhood in the community Jesus left behind, we come first upon a simple adoption of the national, religious formula of the Jews. Both Peter and Stephen call the Jews in their sermons *andres adelphoi* (brothers: Acts 2:29; 7:2); Paul is so addressed by the Jews (13:15), and himself addresses them as such (13:26; 22:1, 22:5; 28:17; compare the interesting text, Romans 9:3, in which the changing of the meaning is clear). However, Acts also refers quite naturally to the Christians as brothers wherever it is the author himself writing (14:2; 28:15).[13] Schelkle considers Jewish those texts of James that use the word *adelphos* (1:9; 2:15; 4:11). Here I think one must say that by "brother" is meant one's fellow Christian, but that in fact the community of James had simply taken over this usage from the Jewish mother church, and that this community had apparently not yet achieved complete separation from Judaism. To this extent we can say that the use of the idea of brother does not here have a markedly Christian stamp.

Its decisive Christian emphasis is the work of Paul for whom it followed naturally from the development of Christianity as something independent of Judaism, which was his life's work. Indeed, the new emphasis

---

[13] Schelkle, *RAC*, II, 636, considers that this text is an example of the Jewish usage; but that it is more appropriately to be regarded as the terminology of the Christian community is shown by A. Wikenhauser in his *Die Apostelgeschichte,* 3rd ed. (Regensburg New Testament, 5), (1956), 285.

in the idea of brother is ultimately a necessary linguistic side effect of this struggle for a concrete historical separating out of the Christian. "Brother", for Paul, is the natural name of one's *Christian* fellow believer, and we find it in a great many texts.[14] The word *pseudadelphos* ("false brother") is actually a word coined by Paul in which he expresses the sad experience of his missionary work and sets the limits of Christian brotherhood.[15] We shall not find a developed theory of Christian brotherhood in Paul, but he does offer a number of important new ideas for it. The most important one is found in Romans 8:14–17, 29:

> For all who are led by the Spirit of God are sons of God. For you did not receive the spirit of slavery to fall back into fear, but you have received the spirit of sonship. When we cry, "Abba! Father!" it is the Spirit himself bearing witness with our spirit that we are children of God, and if children, then heirs, heirs of God and fellow heirs with Christ. . . . For those whom he foreknew he also predestined to be conformed to the image of his Son, in order that he might be the firstborn among many brothers.

Hebrews 2:11 is related to this text: "For he who sanctifies and those who are sanctified have all one origin. That is why he is not ashamed to call them brothers." This provides the theological anchor of the Christian conception of brotherhood. If the brotherhood of Israel

---

[14] These texts can easily be found with the help of a concordance. Schelkle's observation is interesting: the word "brother", though found frequently in the chief epistles, occurs only rarely in the pastoral epistles.

[15] Schelkle, *RAC,* II, 638; see 2 Cor 11:26; Gal 2:4.

depended on the special paternity of God which was given in its election, then in Christianity the idea of fatherhood is made more profound through the Trinity. The fatherhood of God refers in the first place to *the* Son, Christ, and then through him to us, since his Spirit is in us and says "Father" in us (Rom 8:16).[16] The fatherhood of God, then, is a fatherhood mediated to us through Christ in the Spirit. God is primarily the Father of Christ; but we are "in Christ", and are so through the Holy Spirit.[17] We can see here how the Jewish idea of the Father is transformed and intensified in Christianity. Fatherhood, and with it brotherhood, gains a far greater depth of meaning; it points beyond the act of *will* involved in election toward a union which affects our very being.

After we had established that the idea of God the Father was necessary for the conception of brotherhood, we saw that the Adam-Noah-Abraham teaching in Jewish thought was its other anchor. This doctrine, too, is reinterpreted by Paul in a Christian sense, which also had an influence on the idea of brotherhood. In place of the simple Adam story of Genesis—which, moreover, even in its gnostic commutations, had remained a one-Adam story—Paul develops in 1 Corinthians 15 and Romans 5 his doctrine of the two Adams. Christ, having passed through the death of the first Adam, becomes in the Resurrection a new, second Adam, the Father

[16] The close connection between Christ and the Spirit, which is essential for this argument, is stated by Paul in the succinct formula "The Lord is the Spirit" (2 Cor 3:17). See P. van Imschoot's article on "Geist Gottes" ("the Spirit of God") in Haag's *Bibellexikon,* 531–40 (especially 537).

[17] See A. Oepke's article on *en* (in) in the *TWNT,* II, 534–39.

of a new and better humanity. Thus with Christ there begins not only a new humanity, but also a new human brotherhood, which surpasses and replaces the old. For the old brotherhood of Adam is, in the eyes of Paul—who looks back at it from the new Adam, Christ—merely a fraternity of evil and, therefore, not worth seeking after. Only the new brotherhood, which is also universal in its tendency, brings a true unity of salvation. We can see how the doctrine of the two Adams implies a marked criticism of the humanity ideal of the Enlightenment, by accepting only the second humanity, that of the "last man", Christ (1 Cor 15:45). Its brotherhood *is not yet* universal, but it seeks to become so.[18] Men, in general, *are not yet* brothers in Christ, but they can and must become so. While the doctrine of the two Adams, despite its universal tendency, must involve in the concrete a certain limitation of brotherhood (which, however, may never be seen as a closed, but always as an open brotherhood), in the new version of the Abraham doctrine the impression of delimitation predominates. This doctrine had hitherto declared the closed and special nature of Israel, but Paul bursts asunder even this special nature and proclaims as the true children of Abraham, independently of any national privilege, all those who have the faith of Abraham, that is, who are in Christ Jesus (Rom 4; Gal 3:16–29; 4:21–31). Nevertheless, even here the delimitation is not boundless. In place of the national barrier we now have the spiritual barrier between faith and unbelief. It

---

[18] The word "brother" is not used in this connection, but it is an obvious implication through the whole of Paul's thinking at this point.

is important to note that neither Paul nor any other New Testament author founded Christian brotherhood on rebirth, in the sense of the mystery religions; it is certainly a viewpoint possible in a comprehensive account of the implications of New Testament thinking, and we do find it in the Fathers; however, the New Testament itself does not formulate these implications. Perhaps this may be mere chance; nevertheless, it is a fact that is not unimportant for our understanding of the character of New Testament religion. It shows that neither Paul, nor anyone else in the New Testament, understood the Christian community according to the analogy of a mystery brotherhood. This community is far more public than a mystery group. It sees itself not in analogy with the more or less private mystery groups, but in analogy with the people of Israel—indeed, with humanity. It claims to be the true Israel and the germ cell of the new mankind.[19] Its new brotherhood is to be understood from this claim.

From what we have said so far, it is clear that the old problem inherent in the idea of brotherhood is posed again with Paul: the problem of the two zones of ethical attitudes. Despite all delimitation and universalism, the idea of brotherhood is, as we have seen, by no means simply generalized. Every man *can* become a Christian, but only he who really does is a brother. The effect of this situation is shown in the ethical terminology of the apostle. The attitude of agape (love) is appropriate

[19] This public claim of the Church has been worked out particularly by E. Peterson. See his essays "Die Kirche" and "Der Monotheismus als politisches Problem", in *Theologische Traktate* (Munich, 1951), 409–28 and 45–147 respectively.

toward every man, but *philadelphia* (brotherly love) only toward one's fellow Christian.[20] The use of this idea for those other than blood relations seems to be specifically Christian.[21] But it shows very clearly that the Christians together form an inner ring in their ethos, that they are (or should be) held together by a spirit of brotherly love which is even greater than that of the general agape. This idea is clearly expressed in a number of texts, particularly in Galatians 6:10: "Let us do good to all men, and especially to those who are of the household of faith."[22] Closely related to this passage is a text from 1 Peter 2:17: "Honor all men. Love the brotherhood."[23] The brotherhood of Christians, which arises in the first instance from the removal of the barriers of the Jewish fraternal community, fixes its own frontiers with increasing distinctness as the young Church gradually takes charge. Within the brotherhood itself this results in a widespread tearing down of all dividing barriers. The existing social order is not changed, it is true, but the Epistle to Philemon (and also 1 Tim) shows us how unimportant they have become: the Christian master must see his brother in the

[20] H. Schurmann, "Gemeinde als Bruderschaft im Lichte des Neuen Testaments", *Diaspora, Gabe und Aufgabe* (Paderborn, 1955), 21–31 (esp. 27).

[21] Von Soden, 146, 20f.

[22] See also 1 Cor 6:5, 8 and Schurmann, "Gemeinde als Bruderschaft". Many examples are quoted in Sladeczek's article, *"He philadelphia* [brotherly love] nach den Schriften des hl. Apostels Paulus", *TQ,* 76 (1894): 272–95.

[23] For the special Christian meaning of *adelphotes* (the concrete fraternal community) see von Soden, 146, 14f., and Schelkle, *RAC,* II, 638.

Christian slave (Phil 16), and Christian slaves are exhorted not to despise their Christian masters, because their masters are also their brothers (1 Tim 6:2). If we compare these texts with similar passages in Epictetus, the superiority of the limited brotherhood over the general ideal of humanity is clear: it creates a true relationship, whereas the other remains an empty ideal.

In the Johannine writings, the Christian idea of brotherhood finds its final form. Not only is the word "brother" here restricted to one's fellow Christian; it is also particularly striking that John always demands brotherly love, the love of Christians for one another, but never speaks of the love of all men.[24] The communities, which are now distinguishable from all other previous human groupings as something new and different, tend obviously to a certain exclusivity. This is clearly shown by a text such as 3 John, verses 5–8:

> Beloved, it is a loyal thing you do when you render any service to the brothers, especially to strangers, who have testified to your love before the church. You will do well to send them on their journey as befits God's service. For they have set out for his sake and have accepted nothing from the heathen. So we ought to support such men, that we may be fellow workers in the truth.

The separate fraternal communities are here reminded of their mutual brotherliness (cf. 2 Jn 13) and warned against mutual exclusivity, but their being closed against the heathen is accepted, probably with some historical justification. Nevertheless, one senses that there is a

[24] J. Michl in the Regensburg New Testament, 8 (Regensburg, 1953), 287.

danger here for the Christian idea of brotherhood. It has moved beyond the critical stage of indefiniteness but threatens to become too fixed, to lose that openness which it must have from the very nature of the message of Christ.

The Idea of Brotherhood in the Fathers

The word "brother" occurs frequently and as a matter of course in the Fathers up to the third century.[25] The theory of Christian brotherliness is developed in several directions, and material is taken over from the pagan environment. Thus it is baptism which is now regarded as the precise moment at which one becomes a "brother". It represents, as rebirth, the acceptance into the Christian "brotherhood" as the community calls itself.[26] In this rebirth the Church is the Mother and God is the Father.[27] The connection of brotherhood and rebirth involves (perhaps at first uncon-

[25] Schelkle, *RAC*, II, 639f. The usage is found in sepulchre symbolism until the fourth century (see H. Leclerq's article "Frères", *DACL*, V, 2, 2578–85 [esp. 2580ff]).

[26] Tertullian, *De bapt.*, 20, 5 (*CCSL*, I, 295). For the community as *fraternitas*, see *Ap.*, 39, 10 (*CCSL*, I, 151); *De praescr.*, 20, 8 (*CCSL*, I, 202); *De pud.*, 7, 22 (plural) (*CCSL*, II, 1294); *De virg vel.*, 14, 2 (*CCSL*, II, 1223). Since *De am.*, 48, 3 (*CCSL*, II, 854) and *Scorp.*, 8, 4 (*CCSL*, II, 1083), the three youths in the fiery furnace can be described as *trina fraternitas*, Tertullian's idea of the Church as the *corpus trium* could be in the background. See Ratzinger, *Volk und Haus Gottes*, 75f.

[27] *De bapt.*, 20, 5 (*CCSL*, I, 295). On *mater ecclesia* and *fraternitas christianorum* in Cyprian, see Ratzinger, *Volk und Haus Gotte*, 87ff. On the idea of *mater ecclesia* in general, see the plentiful material in H. Rahner, *Mater ecclesia* (Einsiedeln, 1944).

sciously) a certain resemblance to the groups of the
mystery religions, from which—as a further important
formal element—the "secret discipline" is then taken
over.[28] This necessarily meant a further closing of the
ranks of the brotherhood in relation to others, toward
which persecution doubtless contributed. On the other
hand, it also made the inner cohesion into a truly living
brotherhood. As the crux of Christian brotherhood we
always recognize something which is the heart of the
Christian "secret discipline" and, at the same time, the
center given by Jesus to his new people: the eucharistic
meal of brotherhood.[29]

As the persecuted Church was also—and remained—
in the highest degree a missionary Church, we see, parallel with the limitation of the idea of brotherhood just
described, a profound tendency toward delimitation.
Ignatius of Antioch lays stress on a brotherly attitude
toward one's persecutors. In imitation of their guiltless
persecuted Master, Christians must, by their kindness,
show brotherliness toward their oppressors.[30] Tertullian
also explicitly distinguishes the two kinds of brotherhood. One depends on common descent and embraces
all men; the other depends on the common knowledge
of God and the spirit of holiness that is drunk by Chris-

[28] See the article on "secret discipline" in *RAC*, I, 667–76 (O.
Perler); *LTK*, 2nd ed., I, 863f. (O. Perler); *RGG*, 3rd ed., I, 606ff.
(J. Leipoldt).
[29] For the biblical aspect, see F. Kattenbusch, "Der Quellort der
Kirchenidee", *Festgabe A. Harnack zum 70. Geburtstag* (Tubingen,
1921), 143–72; for the patristic, Ratzinger, *Volk und Haus Gottes;*
for the systematic, J. Ratzinger, "Die Kirche als Geheimnis des
Glaubens", *Lebendiges Zeugnis*, I (1956–1957): 19–34.
[30] *Eph.*, 10, 3 (ed. J. A. Fischer, Darmstadt, 1956), 150.

tians in common.[31] In his idea of brotherhood in general, Tertullian was probably influenced by Stoic ideas.[32]

By the third century, however, the word "brother" is found less and less as a designation among Christians. It is instructive for an understanding of the inner development of the Church to see the two ways in which the word finally comes to be used. The first usage we find in Cyprian who no longer employs the word "brother" as a term of address to Christians, except to bishops and clerics.[33] This is no longer the old brotherhood of the faithful; it reminds one rather of the well-known secular idea of the brotherhood of princes with each other[34] which was later to become clearly apparent in the gradations of address for bishops, presbyters, and laymen. The other usage developed in the context of asceticism, in the monastic communities, in which the idea of "brother" and "sister" lived on after it had passed away from a Church which had grown too vast for it to have any concrete meaning.[35] Thus there is a restriction of the idea of brotherhood to the hierarchy and to ascetics, to which actual church life had now become reduced. As we know, this state of affairs has persisted up to our own times, with all its inevitably

[31] *Ap.*, 39, *CCSL*, I, 151 (Schelkle, *RAC*, II, 639).

[32] Schelkle, *RAC*, II, 640.

[33] "It certainly sounds like a formula when Cyprian begins his epistles with '*fratres carissimi*'. In individual address he uses '*frater*' only for bishops and clerics; Cyprian calls only a confessor 'brother' (*Ep.*, 53)" quoted in Schelkle, *RAC*, II, 640.

[34] See F. Dölger, "Bruderlichkeit der Fursten", *RAC*, II, 641–46.

[35] Schelkle, *RAC*, II, 640. See von Soden, 146, 24ff.

damaging effects. Thus historical analysis has led to the point from which our reflection about the Christian idea of brotherhood today—its significance and its possibilities—must start.

TWO

AN ATTEMPT AT SYNTHESIS

Following this brief historical survey, let us now try to define the Christian idea of brotherhood. This Christian idea can be set out in the form of two different arguments, one of a dogmatic nature and one of a moral nature.

The Basis of Christian Brotherhood: Faith

Christian brotherhood, unlike the purely secular brotherhood of Marxism, is, above all, brotherhood based on the common paternity of God. Unlike the impersonal Stoic idea of God the father and the vague paternal idea of the Enlightenment, the fatherhood of God is a fatherhood mediated by the Son and including brotherly union in the Son.

If, therefore, Christian brotherhood is to be vitally realized, both a vital knowledge of the fatherhood of God and a vital joining with Jesus Christ in a unity of grace are necessary.

The fatherhood of God gives Christian brotherhood its firm foundation. It is important here to understand fully the new knowledge that the Christian Faith has given us of God's paternity. Mythical religion, Plato and the Stoics, and eighteenth-century deism all speak of God as a father. And yet it is something quite different when the Christian says "Our Father". Early mythical thought conceived of the sky as the world-creating force which, together with Mother Earth, produced all the life of the world. In this naturalistic sense, then, the sky can be called the "father" of men.[1] Greek philosophy spiritualized this idea without completely removing its basic assumption. In the eternal, transcendent idea of the good, Plato sees the father and the lord, but its quality as "person" remains in doubt, and there is no

---

[1] See G. Schrenk's article on *pater* (father) in *TWNT*, V, 951f.

question of a personal relationship with the creatures of the world.[2] With the Stoics the return to naturalism is quite clear. Their doctrine of the fatherhood of God depends on a reinterpretation in terms of natural philosophy of the old myth of *hieros gamos* (sacred marriage) of Zeus and Hera. Thus it remains ultimately a proposition of natural philosophy when man appears in Epictetus as *idios huios tou theou* (God's own son).[3] It certainly does not mean that he is seen in relation to a personal, caring and loving, angry and forgiving, paternal God. He is merely the culminating point of the cosmos, the one most filled by its sublime powers. The uncosmic, strictly personalist idea of Father, which gives to the paternity of God the seriousness of a true claim on us and to the fraternity of his children life and significance, is revealed only in the words of the Bible and is thus apparent only to the eyes of faith. Insight into the brotherhood of men is given ultimately only to him who has seen, in faith, the full paternity of God.

At the same time the concreteness of God, his personal relation to man, also undergoes an increasing spiritualization in the language of Scripture—an increasing spiritualization which does not, however, lead to increasing rarification (as is always the danger) but, on the contrary, serves to intensify the concreteness and the living reality of his fatherhood. This God never becomes a God of the philosophers; he remains the living God, the God of Abraham, of Isaac, and of Jacob; more, he becomes the God of Jesus Christ and thus the God who has

[2] See the texts quoted in ibid., 954.
[3] *Diss.,* I, 19, 9; Schrenk, 955, 28.

taken on our flesh and blood and our whole human nature. In Jesus Christ, God has not only spoken to men but has also finally and radically made it possible for them to speak to him; for in him God became man and, as man, finally stepped out of his totally different being and entered into the dialogic situation of all men. Jesus the *man* stands as such within the community of discourse which unites all men as beings of the same order. The man Jesus can be addressed by every man, but in him it is God who is addressed. Thus the question of how changeable man can address a totally different, unchangeable God is resolved. In Christ, God has taken a piece of this world's time and of changeable creature-liness, drawn it to himself, and finally thrown open the door between himself and his creatures. In Christ, God has become God more concretely, more personally, and more "addressably", "a partner of men". We are better placed to understand the importance of this for the Christian conception of fatherhood and brotherhood if we consider more closely the biblical growth of the idea. We have already seen that the Old Testament distinguishes two kinds of divine paternity and, correspondingly, two kinds of human childhood: the sonship of all peoples because of creation; the sonship of Israel because of its election. The Old Testament expresses Israel's priority by (among other things) calling Israel the "firstborn son of God" (Ex 4:22).

At the time of the kings an important development takes place in Israel's understanding of itself. The king now became virtually the personification of all Israel; he represented, as it were, its "total person". (Since the research work by Pedersen, this expression of Max

Scheler's can be used to describe Israelite thinking on this question.)[4] Thus the name "the son of God" is transferred to the king (2 Sam 7:14; Ps 2:7; 89:27). He is the son of God in the sense described, inasmuch as he represents Israel, which has a special elective sonship in relation to God. When the idea of a king passed into the eschatological hope of salvation and the idea of the Messiah was formulated concretely, the title of sonship went with it and became an honorific designation for the king of the last times, the Messiah, as the fulfilled image of the true Israel. Exegesis of the last few decades has confirmed the view that nearly all the synoptic texts which call Jesus *huios tou theou* (Son of God) are not to be understood in the sense of a metaphysical statement about the eternal inner-trinitarian divine sonship of Jesus, but reproduce the messianic title of honor, designating him as the epitome of the true Israel.[5] This accords with the fact that Jesus saw himself expressly as the founder of a new Israel already founded in his person—a conception that John expresses by having Jesus describe himself in two places in suggestive imagery as the new Jacob-Israel (Jn 1:51 [cf. Gen 28:12] and 4:6, 11–12).

If we compare these exegetical findings with our dogmatic acknowledgment of the divine sonship of Jesus, we can say that Christ is the fulfillment of what Israel only foreshadowed. He is truly the "Son". Thus he is ultimately the true and real Israel because he possesses

[4] J. Pedersen, *Israel: Its Life and Culture,* I–II (London, 1946).

[5] See, for example, O. Cullmann, *The Christology of the New Testament* (London, 1959), 275–305. Concerning the disputed interpretation of Mk 14:61, see the controversy between Blinzler and Stauffer in *Hochland,* 49 (1956–1957): 563–68.

the highest distinction of Israel, the sonship of God, in an infinitely more real way than was the case with the old People of God. At the same time, the fact that he has himself become a man, "Israel", shows that he does not regard his divine sonship as something reserved only for himself: the meaning of the Incarnation is rather to make what is his available to all. Man can be "in Christ", enter into him, and become one with him; and whoever is in Jesus Christ shares his sonship and is able to say with him, "Abba", "my father".[6] The new Israel, which is composed of all the faithful, is no longer a son merely because of the choosing and sum-moning call of God, the ultimate concrete form of which is the Torah; she is a "son in the son" (Eckhart); she is a son through being planted in the innate Son of the Father (Jn 1:18), with whom we are *one single* body, one single "seed of Abraham". "You are all one in Christ Jesus", Paul emphasizes in Galatians 3:28, after (in 3:16) he had emphasized that the promise given to Abraham did not refer to many, but only to one man, Christ Jesus, with whom, however, we are united in the unity of a single man. Thus the ideas of fatherhood-sonship-brotherhood acquire a completely new ring, the ring of reality. Behind the word "father" there stands the *fact* of our true childhood in Christ Jesus (Gal 4:6; Rom 8:15f.). What is new about the New Testament statements concerning the Father is not a new psycholog-ical atmosphere, nor a new subjective intensity, nor a new idea, but the new fact created by Christ. The mood

[6] According to Quell, 984f., *Abba* is, in fact, an expression that a child would use, almost like "daddy". In any case it expresses the reality of the new child-father relationship.

of trusting love and pure devotion may be found in late Jewish prayers or in the texts of the Hermes mystery cult.[7] But in these it is ultimately *only* a question of atmosphere. What is expressed by them is valuable and profound and can be largely taken over by the Christian. But it acquires in Christianity a new meaning by being founded firmly on fact—the fact of our real embodiment in Christ, which includes our becoming truly sons. What is true of the ideas of "fatherhood" and "sonship" is no less true of "brotherhood". This is the fundamental dogmatic basis for the brotherliness of Christians among one another; for this brotherliness is founded on our being incorporated in Christ Jesus, in the uniqueness of a new man. Like the fatherhood of God, the brotherhood of Christians in the Lord is raised—through the Christ-event—above the realm of ideas to the dignity of true actuality. We also find here the concrete realization and the constant source of Christian brotherliness. It rests on the fact of our being embodied in Christ. The act that does this for us is baptism (which is renewed in penance). The celebration of the Eucharist is the constant reestablishment of our bodily unity with the Lord and with one another. But with this idea we are already on the way toward realizing Christian brotherhood concretely, and that we shall pursue later on. Summing up what we have said so far, we can assert that Christian brotherhood differs from all other brotherhoods that transcend the sphere of blood brotherhood precisely in its character as real and actual. This is grasped in faith and acquired through the sacraments.

[7] Schrenk, 957ff.

From these dogmatic conclusions we can deduce the Christian attitudes which are able to provide the basis for an ethos of true brotherhood. In general terms, these consist, as we have seen, in the conscious spiritual acceptance of the fatherhood of God and union with the life of Christ. We shall now endeavor to explore these two relationships a little further.

Christian brotherhood is ultimately founded on the faith that gives us our assurance of our real sonship in relation to the heavenly Father and of our brotherhood among one another. But here it is necessary to emphasize the social dimension of faith more than is generally done. To take only one example: when theologians today interpret the opening words of the Our Father, they usually restrict themselves to an analysis of the word "father", and this is in tune with our contemporary religious awareness. But a theologian such as Cyprian, on the other hand, chose to give special attention to the word "our".[8] In fact this word does have great importance, for only *one* man has the right to say "*my* Father" to God, and that is Jesus Christ, the only-begotten Son. All other men must say "*our* Father", for the Father is God for us only so long as we are part of the community of his children. For "me" he becomes a Father only through my being in the "we" of his children. The Christian prayer to the Father "is not the call of a soul that knows nothing outside God and itself",[9] but is bound to the community of brothers.

[8] *De dom. or.*, 8, *CSEL*, III, 1 (Hartel), 271f.; see Ratzinger, *Volk und Haus Gottes*, 99.
[9] Ratzinger, ibid.

Together with these brothers we make up the one Christ, in whom and through whom alone we are able to say "Father", because only through Christ and in Christ are we his "children". Thus, strictly speaking, we should not say that Christ taught men to call God "Father", but rather that it was he who taught them to say *"Our* Father"—and the "Our" is no less important than the "Father", for it *locates* faith and prayer, assigning them their christological component. When we see this, Harnack's view[10] that the "Son" does not form part of the gospel proclaimed by Christ is shown to be obviously false. Its place is firmly fixed in the word "our" and, in a logically developing *kerygma,* could not fail to emerge as the social dimension of faith. It is important that this social dimension should once more be brought to the consciousness of the faithful, that Christian belief in God the Father should be shown necessarily to involve the affirmation of our brothers, the brotherhood of all Christians.

Living faith in the spirit of the Our Father will necessarily lead to a new relationship to God and to our fellow man, whom we recognize as our brother. Toward God it includes the attitudes of trust and of love. God has accepted us as his children in Christ Jesus and has thus become our Father; he is the absolutely faithful and dependable God who has remained true to his covenant in spite of the sin of men—indeed, has been moved by this sin and faithlessness to an even greater outpouring of grace and forgiveness. He is the exact opposite of the Homeric "father of the gods and of men". That

[10] A. von Harnack, *What is Christianity?* 5th ed. (London, 1958), 95ff.

god was a domineering and unpredictable despot—not despite his fatherhood, but precisely because of it: there is a despotic quality in the Greek idea of fatherhood.[11] And yet this despotic father was not himself the highest power, for above, or beside him, stood *moira* (fate) and *themis* (the law of the cosmos), against which even he could do nothing.[12] Against this background the biblical idea of fatherhood acquires its true greatness. For this God is the ultimate power, power itself, *Pantocrator,* and, at the same time, the most reliable, unfailing fidelity. Both these qualities are able to move man to an ultimate, unshakable trust that is love and worship in one.

A second attitude which faith produces in us is in relation to our fellow men. One might call it, with Dietrich von Hildebrand, "the true loss of oneself".[13] To become a Christian means to become incorporated in the Son, in Christ, so that we become "sons in the Son". This is a sacramental, but also an ethical process. Its ethical nature is illuminated by one of Eckhart's thoughts, which, when taken to its logical conclusion, is dogmatically incorrect but can still help us to see the present point more clearly. Eckhart interprets the dogmatic teaching that Christ possessed human nature, but not human personality, wrongly by saying that, in that case, Christ was "man in general", possessing humanity without any individuality or particular qualities. In one of his German sermons he expresses the

[11] Schrenk, 952f.

[12] Ibid., 952f. See also Schmid, *Matthaus,* 126.

[13] D. von Hildebrand, *Die Umgestaltung in Christus* (Einsiedeln, 1950), 326–38.

doctrine of the two natures and the one person like this: "The eternal Word did not take upon himself this or that man, but rather did it take upon itself a free, undivided human nature."[14] This is an ethical reinterpretation of the doctrine of the hypostatic union. Eckhart seeks to make the dogmatic statement yield a basic ethical principle. For Christ is the goal of man, nay more: it is for man to be himself "in Christ", to grow into Christ. To the question of how man can grow into Christ, Eckhart's suggestion offers a surprisingly clear and simple answer. Christ is man, humanity free from any particular individuality. Accordingly, man grows into Christ the more that he becomes "man in himself"—the more that he loses himself, his own particular ego. What separates him from Christ is his own individuality, the self-assertion of his ego. What unites him with Christ is his general humanity. The measure of his share in the hypostatic union, his being "in Christ", is the extent to which he has destroyed his own ego; so that, according to Eckhart, if he were able to rid himself entirely of his ego, he would become identical with Christ. It is not necessary here to enter on a discussion of this ethic, which is an ethic of the mystical body of Christ and yet runs the danger of turning into pure humanism. The important thing here is to see the truth that lies at the heart of it: to become one with Christ means to lose one's "oneself", to cease to regard one's own ego

---

[14] The axiom "assumpsit naturam", Sermones de tempore, VI, 2, 57, in Meister Eckhart, Lateinische Werke, IV (ed. Benz-Decker-Koch [Stuttgart, 1956]), 56f. The quoted text from the 47th German sermon, 158, 1–3, can be found on p. 57, n. 1, together with a large number of further parallel texts. See also for the whole, Ratzinger, Volk und Haus Gottes, 234ff. (esp. 235).

as an absolute. It is consistent with this basic view that Eckhart's ethic has a marked social character and emphasizes the service of our neighbor rather than the joys of contemplation.[15] The belief that we have all become a single new man in Jesus Christ will always call us to let the separating particularity of our own egos, the self-assertion of human selfhood, melt into the community of the new man Jesus Christ. Whoever believes in Jesus Christ has not only found an ethical model to be imitated privately but is called to break up his own merely private ego and merge into the unity of the body of Christ.

The ethic of Christ is essentially an ethic of the body of Christ. Inevitably, therefore, it means losing one's own ego and becoming one in brotherhood with all those who are in Christ. As an ethic of true self-loss, it necessarily includes the brotherhood of all Christians.

[15] For the social character of Eckhart's mysticism, see H. Piesch, *Meister Eckharts Ethik* (Lucerne, 1935), 111–22; and O. Karrer, *Meister Eckhart* (Munich, 1926), 189–93.

The Removal of Barriers within the Brotherhood of Christians

Union with Christ includes the union of Christians among one another, and thus involves a removal of the separating barriers of nature and history. Therefore the ethos of a brotherhood with equal rights must transcend the necessary divisions of class or hierarchic order.

The removal of barriers that had before seemed insurmountable is an essential part of the Christian experience of newness. "From now on, therefore, we regard no one from a human point of view; even though we once regarded Christ from a human point of view, we regard him thus no longer. Therefore, if any one is in Christ, he is a new creation; the old has passed away, behold, the new has come" (2 Cor 5:16–17). All previous differences lost their importance before the revolutionary reality of this new creation. The great unbridgeable difference which had divided the world now lost its meaning—the difference between Israel and the heathen, between pure and impure, between elect and nonelect.

Remember that you were at that time separated from Christ, alienated from the commonwealth of Israel, and strangers to the covenant of promise, having no hope and without God in the world. But now in Christ Jesus you who once were afar off have been brought near in the blood of Christ. For he is our peace, who has made

57

us both one, and has broken down the dividing wall of hostility, . . . that he might . . . reconcile us both to God in one body through the cross, thereby bringing the hostility to an end. And he came and preached peace to you who were far off and peace to those who were near . . . (Eph 2:12–17; cf., in this context, the vision of Peter before the baptism of Cornelius, Acts 10:9–16).

In Ephesians, the word "mystery" means specifically this miracle of the union of Jews *and* Gentiles in the one body of Christ.[1] The mystery of Christ is the mystery of the removal of barriers. Other texts in Paul develop this idea: "For as many of you as were baptized into Christ have put on Christ. There is neither Jew nor Greek, there is neither slave nor free, there is neither male nor female; for you are all one in Christ Jesus", says Galatians 3:27–28, placing the removal of the religious differences between Jew and Gentile side by side with that of the basic social differences between slave and free man, between man and woman. We may note in this connection that, in contrast to the mystery religions, it is an exclusively Christian idea that "a 'sister' has the right to stand as an equal beside her 'brother'."[2]

Colossians goes even further by including national barriers with the religious and social barriers that are removed by Christ. "Put on the new nature, which is being renewed in knowledge after the image of its creator. Here there cannot be Greek and Jew, circumcized and uncircumcized, barbarian, Scythian, slave, free man,

[1] G. Bornkamm's article on *mysterion* in *TWNT*, IV, 827. See H. Schlier's "Die Einheit der Kirche im Denken des Apostels Paulus", *Cath*, X, 1 (1954): 14–26; also his *Der Brief an die Epheser* (Dusseldorf, 1957), 61.

[2] Schelkle, *RAC*, II, 638.

but Christ is all, and in all" (Col 3:10–11). Before and above all these statements about the removal of barriers stand the inexorable words of the Lord to the rich young ruler: "Why do you call me good? No one is good but God alone" (Mk 10:18). They acknowledge only one true barrier: that between Creator and creature. Before it all other differences become unimportant.

We recapture here the unique and irrevocable experience of newness which is bound up with the early growth of Christianity and its overcoming of barriers. And yet the abiding actuality of what is said is also apparent in many ways. For example, the overcoming of nationalism is a task that every generation sets itself anew; and, in an age in which Europe is at last striving to break free from the internecine enmity of the past and to achieve unity, it is becoming ever more important. It is equally apparent that our age no longer regards differences of class as ultimate, but seeks to remove them in a spirit of Christian brotherhood. Perhaps, however, it is valuable to consider in a little more detail one question which a Catholic in particular might ask himself in this connection: that of the ethos of hierarchic differences. None of the Pauline texts we have quoted refers to it, but we have the words of Christ (Mt 23:8–11):

> But you are not to be called rabbi, for you have one teacher, and you are all brethren. And call no man your father on earth, for you have one Father, who is in heaven. Neither be called masters, for you have one master, the Christ. He who is greatest among you shall be your servant. (See also the important text of Mt 20:25–28.)

If we take the preceding verses (1–8) as well, it is clear that the false hierarchism and dignity of office cultivated

by the Jews is contrasted with the undifferentiated brotherliness of Christians. And one cannot avoid the serious
challenge that this text puts to us: Does not our actual
Christian reality resemble more the Jewish hierarchism
castigated by Jesus than the picture he gave of Christian
brotherhood? In his book on apostleship, Schelkle takes
up a point from this text and says:

> Thus the Lord's saying takes exception to any man's
> being addressed in the Church as father in spirit. And
> if the saying is preserved in the gospel, then this probably
> really proves that the Church of that time did not award
> the title "father" to anyone but God. . . . Granted that
> by the testimony of their writings Paul and other apostles
> feel like fathers of the faithful, granted too that the expres-
> sion became a regular form of address and exists as such
> even today, . . . still, such a practice always finds its
> meaning, its value, indeed its limitation, in Matthew
> 23:9. May a man claim to be related to another in spiritual
> paternity or maternity? Do not such right and such hon-
> our really belong to God alone . . . ?[3]

One is obliged to add that not only the title of "father"
is qualified by this text, but the whole *external* (and I
mean *external*) form of hierarchism that has developed
over the centuries.

There are a few further observations that might be
made. The New Testament clearly differentiates the authorized representative who continues the mission of
Jesus in an official capacity from the ordinary believers
who are not so authorized.[4] What we call "the hierarchy"

---

[3] K. H. Schelkle, *Discipleship and Priesthood* (London, 1966), 44f.
[4] Of the vast literature on the question of office in the Church,
let us mention here an impressive Protestant publication which shows

and "the priesthood" are New Testament realities. A Catholic theologian will need to lay great emphasis on this, but he has no reason to conceal the fact that the New Testament has its own particular verbal usage. It never calls the officials "priests", or the office "office" The Greek words for office (*arkhe, exousia, time, telos*) are not, for the New Testament, appropriate descriptions for the offices of the Church.

> The New Testament knows these words, but does not employ them in the realm of the Church; rather it draws on the word *diakonia*. *Arkhe* is restricted in New Testament usage to the authority of synagogue and state or to the angelic powers, *time* to the dignity of office of the Old Testament high priest. The result of such lexicographical investigation is impressive enough evidence that office in the Church is an institution essentially ordered to service. The result also makes manifest the self-understanding of the New Testament that order and law mean essentially different things in the Church and in the world. Therefore they cannot be named with the same words.[5]

This final statement is central. One can in no way identify the New Testament office, which is in fact New Testament service, with the phenomenon of priesthood in other religions. It is by nature something totally different. That it resembles priesthood factually, purely as a phenomenon, does not derive from its nature, but from

---

its authorized representative character as based on the New Testament: O. Linton, "Kirche und Amt im Neuen Testament", *Ein Buch von der Kirche*, 110–44.

[5] Schelkle, *Discipleship*, 39n.

the fact that a perfect fulfillment of being in the world of concrete appearances always remains impossible. It comes from a breaking in of the individual element which is not of Christ. So it is that, to this day, the sixth sacrament is called, in the language of the Church, not *sacerdotium,* but *ordo.*

There is a further historical point to be made. The special character of the Christian office emerges with particular clarity when we compare the Christian apostle with his direct parallels in the history of religion, the rabbi and the *theios anthropos* ("man of God") of the Greeks. Both the latter have their own authority, whereas the essential thing for an apostle is to be a servant of Christ and, like Christ, to live by the motto, "My teaching is not mine, but his who sent me" (Jn 7:16).[6] Thus the sense of mission for the rabbi and the "man of God" is an awareness of self; for the apostle it is an awareness of service. "The rabbi's pupil has the goal of becoming a master himself. But for Jesus' disciple, discipleship is not a beginning; it is the fulfillment and destination of his life. He always remains a disciple."[7]

We might add that, as a "father", he still remains a "brother"; his fatherly office is a form of brotherly service, and nothing else. We are here at the point from which we can see the positive element in the Protestant understanding of Christianity, such as we find in Bultmann and in the whole "theology of crisis" preceding

[6] See K. H. Rengstorf's article on *apostolos* in *TWNT,* I, 406–16 (esp. 408ff.); and Schelkle, *Discipleship,* 24f. For Jn 7:16 see the splendid exegesis of it by Augustine, *Tr. in Joh.,* XXIX, 3–5, *CCSL,* 36, 285f.

[7] Schelkle, *Discipleship,* 24.

him. We can agree here with E. Wolf in the closing sentence of his article on the historical development of Christianity: "Christianity is ultimately not a cultural achievement, or an ideology, or the solution of the problems of humanity, or even in its essence 'religion,' but rather the crisis of all religions in Christ."[8] This is an element in Christianity that cannot be lightly set aside. By removing all barriers it continually places the actual differentiations within the Church within this crisis, compelling us to purify them ever anew from within and fill them with the spirit of the same brotherhood that made us "all one in Christ Jesus" (Gal 3:28).

[8] *RGG*, I, 1705.

The Limits of the
Brotherly Community

Christianity does not mean the removal of all barriers, but itself creates a new barrier, that between Christians and non-Christians. Consequently the Christian is the brother of his fellow Christian, but not of the non-Christian. His commitment to love is independent of this, however, and is directed toward anyone in need whom he can help. Nevertheless, the building up and cultivation of a vital inner Christian brotherhood remains one of his chief concerns.

Here we come upon a decisive difference between the Catholic and the Protestant understandings of Christianity. That Christianity has in fact created a limited religious community separate from other groups—the Church—is clear. The question is: How long has this limitation existed, and how legitimate is it?[1] The first question has already been answered in our historical analysis in which we found that as early as Paul there

[1] We can merely mention here the interesting new formulation of these much-discussed questions by W. Kamlah, *Christentum und Geschichtlichkeit. Untersuchungen zur Entstehung des Christentums und zu Augustins "Bürgerschaft Gottes"* (Stuttgart, 1951). Naturally there is no suggestion that Protestant theologians have only one view on this subject—the variety of their positions is well-known—but an "eschatological", anti-institutional view of the Church is widely held by Protestants today and is rooted in their fundamental religious attitude.

was already a clear differentiation of the Christian communities and that an inner Christian ethos had developed. The second question—the question of its legitimacy—is more or less identical with the basic question of how the Catholic idea of the Church is to be justified, and that question cannot be treated here in full. Nevertheless, in our analysis of the ethos of brotherhood among the early Christians we shall see that it is based on the assumption of a closed brotherly community. Hence the nature of this ethos is important for our knowledge of the self-understanding of early Christianity. Finally, we must not forget that Jesus himself did not describe everyone as his brothers and sisters, but only those who were one with him in their assent to the will of the Father (Mk 3:33–34). Only in the parable of the last judgment (Mt 25:31–46) is the idea of brotherhood separated from the idea of unity in the will of the Lord and applied to all those in need, for these are called brothers of the Son of Man who governs the world (but not automatically brothers of believers). But even that is not a judgment on them so much as on the claim each of them has on the love of Christians. With the choosing of the Twelve, the patriarchs of the new Israel, to whom Jesus gives the name "brothers", a special, separate community had already in fact been created.

Let us also remember that Jesus has predicted to his disciples the collapse and failure of all earthly brotherhood and family love: "Brother will deliver up brother to death, and the father his child, and children will rise against parents and have them put to death" (Mt 10:21). But he had also promised them, in the midst of all persecution, a new brotherly community in this world (Mk 10:30). His disciples were not to remain homeless even in this world and in spite of their renunciation of all earthly habitation. The brotherhood of all Christians was coming.

Thus it is only Christians who are true brothers—the others are called *hoi exo,* those who stand outside (1 Th 4:10–12; cf. 1 Cor 5:12, 13; Col 4:5).[2] Only this limited application of the idea of brotherhood is Christian; removal of this barrier was an essentially unrealizable ideal of the Enlightenment. Only within this limitation is the idea of brotherhood a practical possibility. Again the critical question arises: Is it realizable, even so? Or are the borders too widely drawn? Is not the Church too large, too vast for her to be a true community of brothers?

Here we must go back to the original Christian meaning of *ekklesia,* which at first meant the actual realization within the particular local community of the one Church.[3] Brotherhood can first be realized only within the local community—within the particular parish. Heinz Schürmann has pointed out that the question of the size of the parish community ought to be governed by this. It should be possible for everyone to know everyone else. "For you cannot live in brotherhood with someone that you don't even know."[4] One may go on to ask how the brotherhood of parishioners can be achieved in practice. Again a consideration of the original

[2] See Sladeczek, 273 and 291.
[3] See K. L. Schmidt's article on *ekklesia* in *TWNT,* III, 503ff.; F. Kattenbusch, "Der Quellort der Kirchenidee", 170–72; A. Wikenhauser, *Die Kirche als der mystische Leib Christi nach dem Apostel Paulus* (Munster, 1937), 4–13.
[4] "Gemeinde als Bruderschaft", 23.

meaning of *ekklesia* can help us. The word not only means "Church" and "local community", but it can also mean "religious assembly". These three meanings are not simply distinct, unrelated to each other, but are, in fact, much more three levels of a single meaning and, consequently, often overlap with one another. They are connected in the following way: the one Church always exists concretely in the concrete local community. The local community realizes itself as the Church in the religious assembly, that is, above all in the celebration of the Eucharist.[5] Consequently, Christian brotherhood demands concretely the brotherhood of the individual parish community. This brotherhood has its source and center in the celebration of the eucharistic mysteries. In fact, in the classical theology of the Church, the Eucharist has been seen not so much as the soul's meeting with Christ, but rather as the *concorporatio cum Christo*—as the Christians' becoming one in the one body of the Lord.[6] A celebration of the Eucharist that is to be the source of brotherhood must both be inwardly recognized and performed as a sacrament of brotherhood and also externally appear to be such. The recognition that *ekklesia* (Church) and *adelphotes* (brotherhood) are the same thing, that the Church that fulfills herself in the celebration of the Eucharist is essentially a community of brothers, compels us to celebrate the Eucharist as a rite of brotherhood in responsory dialogue—and

[5] Kattenbusch, 170ff. See also Wikenhauser, 11ff.

[6] This is developed in Ratzinger, *Volk und Haus Gottes.* See also F. Hofmann, "Glaubensgrundlagen der liturgischen Erneuerung", *Fragen der Theologie heute,* ed. Feiner-Trutsch-Bockle (Einsiedeln, 1957), 487–517.

not to have a lonely hierarchy facing a group of laymen each one of whom is shut off in his own missal or other devotional book. The Eucharist must again become visibly the sacrament of brotherhood in order to be able to achieve its full, community-creating power. This does not imply a social dogmatism: the vocation of the individual Christian can often be fulfilled quietly in a life of retirement. But even a vocation like this is a form of brotherly service and, therefore, far from invalidating the brotherly nature of the community rite of the Church, further confirms it.

Consideration of the Eucharist takes us a step farther, too. Its celebration originally comprised, of course, both the liturgical meal and an ordinary, "physical" meal shared by Christians meeting together in one large unit.[7] The liturgy and ordinary living had not yet become separated. This situation cannot be reconstructed under present circumstances, but Schürmann rightly points out that the need still remains for parishes to develop appropriate forms of community life outside the liturgy in order to supplement the liturgical gathering and make possible direct brotherly contact.[8] These forms will vary according to circumstances, but we may make one general point: inasmuch as brotherhood in the parish is, as it were, divided up among different societies or organizations, it is necessary to keep bringing people together in larger groups in order to emphasize their relationship to the greater unity of the parish. The individual organi-

[7] H. Schurmann's "Die Gestalt der urchristlichen Eucharistiefeier", *MTZ*, 6 (1955), 107–31, and the literature listed there.
[8] "Gemeinde als Bruderschaft", 24f.

zation is justified only insofar as it serves the brotherhood of the whole community. This aim of making the parish community a true brotherhood ought to be taken very seriously. Today a trade union or a party can exist as a live and fraternal community, and so the actual experience of brotherhood for all the Christian members of a parish community can and, therefore, should become a primary goal. It would be a universal experience which transcended all barriers, of course, for in every parish there are men of different professions and often of different languages and nationalities. It is this universality which gives the parish a superior position to an organization based on any other community of interests. And the parishes ought to come to see one another as sisters, according to the words of John's second Epistle (5:13)— sisters who, in the fellowship of their faith and love, build up together the great unity of the Mother Church, the body of the Lord.

A final question deserves attention: that of the relationship of the Christian community to those outside it. To begin with, it can do no harm to underline once again that this "outside" does indeed exist—that there really are people who are not brothers or not yet brothers. On this point we are always inclined to think more in rationalist eighteenth-century terms than in Pauline and Christian terms; and so we tend to dislike any line of demarcation. In fact, however, the Christian line of demarcation ultimately serves a universal openness, as we shall see. There must, first of all, be a limitation, the formation of a definite, tangible brotherly community which raises the whole from empty romanticism to the level of concrete realizability. Thus it is understandable that apostolic prescriptions for the relationship toward "outsiders" are in part open, but also in part definitive of the frontier. They are open when Paul demands total serving love toward anyone who approaches a Christian needing his help (Rom 13:8; 1 Th 3:12; 5:15; Titus 3:2; also 1 Cor 9:19),[9] when the Christian is told to pray for all men (1 Tim 2:1), to respect non-Christian authority (Rom 13:1ff.; Titus 3:1; cf. 1 Tim 6:1, 2; Titus 2:9; Eph 6:5; Col 3:22ff.; also 1 Pet 2:13–18), and to show himself by his whole being a true benefactor of the world (Phil 2:15ff.; Rom 12:17; 2 Cor 8:21; 1 Th 4:12; 5:22; Rom 15:2; 1 Tim 4:12). Above all, Paul does not see it as any part of his business and, hence, of any Christian's "to sit in judgment on the moral state and the eternal lot of those who are outside the church community. 'For what have I to do with judging outsiders? . . . God judges those outside' (1 Cor 5:12, 13)."[10] Behind this attitude of respect for the spiritual integrity of a non-Christian there is also a sense of keeping within proper bounds. It is expressed more explicitly in Colossians 4:5: "Conduct yourselves wisely towards outsiders."

This wisdom will also dictate caution lest the Christian in self-surrender for the good of the world may himself fall away from his life in God. . . . Again and again the Christian must remind himself of his basic opposition to the world and honestly answer, in every specific situation, the question: "What has a believer in common with

[9] For the whole subject, see the careful research of Sladeczek, 288–95, where every statement by St. Paul about the Christian attitude to *hoi exo* is collected and tabulated. I am indebted to Sladeczek for this whole section.

[10] Ibid., 292.

an unbeliever?" (2 Cor 6:15). Apart from the correct
fulfilment of duty toward all, and apart from the showing
of love toward our neighbors, . . . the Christian must
seek no share or fellowship with unbelievers.[11]

For this reason Christians must strive for the greatest
possible independence from non-Christians[12] and not
choose them for their habitual companions.[13] In fact,
they should have as little as possible to do with them
(2 Cor 6:17).[14]

In attempting to transfer such statements from their
original setting into the present, we are faced with the
difficult question of where the frontier of Christian
brotherhood is today. Does the brotherly community
of the parish consist of all those who are baptized and
are registered officially as Catholics, or can one call
true brothers only the practicing Catholics? This question is difficult to answer because it has no direct analogy
in Paul, and the existence of nonbelieving Christians
on the scale of the present day was at that time unknown.
And yet the situation did arise. Paul coined the word

[11] Ibid., 293f.

[12] Ibid., 294, points 7 and 8. Sladeczek shows here that, according
to Eph 4:28, 1 Th 4:11, and 2 Th 3:12, the Christian should care
for his own bodily needs and reduce them to the essential so that
he does not have to approach someone outside (1 Th 4:12). The
text 1 Cor 7:23 ("Do not become *douloi ton anthropon*") Sladeczek
interprets from 1 Cor 7:21 (*ei kai dunasai eleutheros genesthai, mallon
khresai*) and 1 Cor 3:3, 4 (a synonymous use of *anthropos* and *sarkikos*)
as meaning that Christians should not place themselves at the service
of non-Christians. The warning of 2 Cor 6:14 could mean that
Christians should not have any common business with unbelievers.

[13] Ibid., 294, no. 9: Eph 5:6–7.

[14] For further texts, see ibid., 294f.

pseudadelphos to describe it.[15] If one ignores the pejorative element in the term and, in accordance with what we have said above, refrains from judging the conscience of the other, then one may say that this is the Pauline category for the nonbelieving Christian. Concerning the position of such people to Christ, and thus to the community, Saint Paul says, "Any one who does not have the Spirit of Christ does not belong to him" (Rom 8:9).

This would appear to justify the view that it is only participation in the eucharistic liturgical assembly that makes a person a true member of the Christian fraternal community. If a man never takes part in the brotherly meal of Christians, he cannot be considered as belonging to the brotherhood. The brotherly community of the Christians consists of those, and only those, who come with at least a certain regularity to share in the eucharistic celebration. Only this definition is Pauline, and only this definition is realistic. For only on this view can we hope, with any justification, for an actual realization of a conscious brotherly community. This does not mean, of course, that we should write off those who have been baptized but who have lost the living faith and, therefore, any direct sharing in Christian brotherhood. On the contrary, it means that we must rid ourselves of a dangerous illusion that can easily prevent us from recognizing the true measure of our responsibility toward those whose brothers we could be, but unfor-

[15] Schelkle, *RAC,* II, 638. There is a thorough analysis of the idea in Sladeczek, 279–88 (particularly 279–81). If one wanted to apply the word in the sense suggested to the present situation, one could probably best translate it as "Christian in name only".

tunately all too little are. Moreover, the relation of those who are Christians in name only (*pseudadelphoi*) to the Christian fraternal community is different from that of those totally outside it. Paul exhorts Christians to practice truth and kindness toward them in teaching and preaching,[16] to continue to show them the light of the Word. Only when this is fruitless does he advise breaking off relations with them, keeping out of their way (1 Tim 6:5; 2 Cor 6:17; Rom 16:17; 1 Cor 5:9, 11; 2 Th 3:14; 2 Tim 3:5; Titus 3:10; 2 Th 3:14), and even in extreme cases excluding them formally from the community (1 Cor 5:13). But the goal always remains that their hearts should be changed and that they should be brought back fully into the brotherly community of Christians (2 Cor 2:6–11).[17]

[16] Sladeczek, 281–86.
[17] Ibid., 286ff.

True Universalism

The separating off of the limited Christian brotherhood is not the creation of some esoteric circle, but is intended to serve the whole. The Christian brotherly community does not stand against the whole, but for it. The brotherhood of Christians fulfills its responsibility for the whole through missionary activity, through agape, and through suffering.

If the foundation of the Church, and thus the realization of Christ's mission, has created a new duality among men—that of the Church and the non-Church—then it is clear that the real goal of the work of Jesus refers not to the part, but to the whole—to total humanity.[1] This healing of the whole takes place, according to the will of God, in the dialectical antithesis of the few and the many, in which the few are the starting point from which God seeks to save the many. This basic connection has never been so clearly expressed as in the election doctrine of Karl Barth, whose basic ideas we shall briefly summarize here.[2]

Barth's primary insight is that election has to be under-

---

[1] This is particularly clear in Rom 5:12–21. See the *polloi* of Mk 10:45 par. and Mk 14:24 par.

[2] Karl Barth, *Church Dogmatics*, 2, 2, (Edinburgh, 1958). The following paragraphs are indebted to H. U. von Balthasar, *The Theology of Karl Barth* (San Francisco: Ignatius Press, 1992), 174–88. As we are not concerned here with an exegesis of Barth himself, I have merely drawn out the appropriate lines of his thinking and related them to our present problem.

stood christologically—in terms of salvation history.
It is not an event which takes place between a terrifying
divine absolute on the one side and an isolated creature
on the other, but one which in every case passes concretely through Christ. Whereas a theory of election
that disregards this must operate with two unknowns—
God and man—in Christ the two unknowns become
known. For in Christ what God is—he is grace—becomes visible; at the same time, what man is—he who
experiences grace which releases him from guilt—also
becomes visible. This becomes even clearer in the historical mission of Christ. Jesus Christ, himself innocent,
is chosen to expiate the guilt of the world and in this
sense to be the object of divine rejection, that is, to
bear the fate of rejection which otherwise would befall
all other men. Thus the predestination of Christ is in
quite a new sense *praedestinatio gemina*. This expression,
originally coined by Gottschalk and taken up again by
Calvin, meant for the latter the division of mankind,
a twofold predestination—that to salvation, and that
to damnation. Barth takes this idea of Calvin's and trans-
forms it. For Jesus Christ, the only one worthy of salvation, now takes its complete opposite, the *whole* of
damnation, on himself in a sacred exchange. "In the
election of Jesus Christ, which is the eternal will of
God, God has ascribed to man the former, election,
salvation, and life; and to himself he has ascribed the
latter, reprobation, perdition, and death."[3] In other
words, in the normal course of events God must damn
the sinner and elect the just man; in Christ, however,

---

[3] Barth, *Church Dogmatics*, 2, 2, 187. See also von Balthasar, *Theology of Karl Barth*, 175–76.

there takes place the paradoxical miracle of grace which reverses this: he who alone is just and thus alone is chosen (because the only one worthy), Christ, becomes rejected, takes the fate of the rejection of all upon himself, and thus renders all in his place—in him and through him—elected, just as he had become rejected in us and through us. *Praedestinatio gemina* no longer means, as in Calvin and perhaps even in Gottschalk, that a part of humanity is predestined to happiness and the other to damnation; it means, rather, that God passes the sentence of damnation on himself in Christ and thus makes free for us the place of election, to which then, through our salvation, Christ himself also returns. The will of God in election is therefore double, but not twofold.[4]

From this point we can take a further step which brings us back to our theme. What took place with Jesus Christ, the exchange in the history of election, is not limited to him alone, but is reflected, according to Barth, in the history of creation (in the dualities of light and darkness, earth and water—a somewhat doubtful theory), and is seen, above all, in salvation history.

> To choose one person always means not choosing another. Yet, at the same time, this chosen one, Christ, has been chosen for the sake of those not chosen, and he vicariously bears their fate in his destiny. In this way those not chosen become in truth the elect, while the one elected is rejected for the sake of the others.[5]

Barth rightly points out the great antithetical pairs of salvation history whom we encountered when we

[4] Barth, 2, 2, 171.
[5] Von Balthasar, 112.

were analyzing the Old Testament idea of brotherhood: Cain and Abel, Ishmael and Isaac, Esau and Jacob.[6] The history of these pairs of brothers has only a provisional ending in the rejection of one and the election of the other. Jesus' parable of the prodigal son, which might perhaps be better called his parable of the two brothers, and the doctrine of the two peoples that Paul develops in Romans 9–11 bring about the great reversal: rejection now in the last analysis leads directly to election—the rejected man is now chosen in his very rejection.

Of course, it makes all the difference in the world whether one is chosen or rejected; but both groups have their actual existence only in him. Only in Christ, who is originally both the Elected and the Rejected One, does the opposition between the two camps possess its necessity. Not only is the relativity of their contrast founded in him, so too is the fact that in their very opposition they are yet *brothers,* mutually entangled with one another in their lives and actions, and forming an ineffable and indissoluble unity. Just as the election of Jesus Christ precisely finds its scope in his vicarious reprobation and, conversely just as his vicarious rejection is precisely the confirmation of his election, so too do the elect and repro-

---

[6] Von Balthasar, 182. (Barth also mentions a number of other pairs who are not, however, so important: Saul and David, the two prophets of 1 Kings 13, the two robbers on the cross, and Judas and Paul. He crowns the whole with an interpretation of the relationship between synagogue and Church. See also H. Fries, "Kirche als Ereignis. Zu Karl Barths Lehre von der Kirche", *Cath.,* 11, 2 [1958]: 81–107.)

bate stand not only over against each other but also next to each other and live for each other.[7]

In other words, the mystery of this vicariousness, given in Christ and forming the basis of all election, is carried out from Christ according to the will of God in a whole system of vicarious relationships throughout salvation history as its fundamental law. Just as Christ, the chosen one, became in a sacred exchange the one rejected for us in order to confer on us his election, this exchange relationship recurs constantly in salvation history following him. Again and again he who is chosen, called by grace to the knowledge of faith and of love, must be ready to be vicariously rejected, so that through him another can be chosen also. One stands in the place of the other, and it is an expression of God's faith in us that he draws us into this system of vicarious election.

This takes us a step further. Ultimately this system cannot be based on individuals alone but finds its comprehensive framework in the antithesis of Church and non-Church, of *laos* and *oulaos*. The Church, as such and as a whole, is the bearer of this vicarious election, the highest mission of which is to become vicarious rejection. The task of the Church and of the individual Christian is a dynamic one. Just as the individual who is chosen can never cut himself off from those whom he thinks are not, so the Church, as a chosen community, cannot cut herself off from those who are not God's people. Election is always, at bottom, election for others.

---

[7] Von Balthasar, 181.

For the Church as for the individual, election is identical with the missionary obligation. The Church is, therefore, "an *open* space, a dynamic concept; from the outset. For all its visibility, the earthly Church is but the movement of the Kingdom of God into the world in the sense of an eschatological totality."[8] In relation to Christian brotherhood this means that, however important it is for the Church to grow into the unity of a single brotherhood, she must always remember that she is only one of two sons, one brother beside another, and that her mission is not to condemn the wayward brother, but to save him. The Church, it is true, must unify herself to form a strong inner brotherhood in order to be truly *one* brother. But she does not seek to be *one* brother in order finally to shut herself off from the other; rather she seeks to be one brother because only in this way can she fulfill her task toward the other, living for whom is the deepest meaning of her existence, which itself is grounded wholly in the vicarious existence of Jesus Christ.

And so at last we arrive at the Christian answer to the question of the idea of brotherhood raised at the beginning: the problem of the two zones of ethical behavior. In contrast to the Stoics and the Enlightenment, Christianity affirms the existence of the two different zones and calls only fellow believers "brothers". On the other hand, however, Christianity, unlike the mystery cults, is wholly free from a desire to form some self-sufficient esoteric group. Rather the separating off of some has its ultimate significance only in the service it fulfills for the others who are, at bottom,

[8] Von Balthasar, 183.

the "other brother" and whose fate is in the hands of the first brother. We can therefore be certain that the Church will gain in missionary power as she begins to make her own internal brotherliness more vital.[9]

There remains the task of defining more closely the concrete, day-to-day manner of Christian service toward the "other" brother. The first obligation laid on a Christian is that of missionary activity, and here again there is a certain dialectic which needs to be taken seriously. On the one hand stands the public commission of Christ: "What I tell you in the dark, utter in the light; and what you hear whispered, proclaim upon the housetops" (Mt 10:27). This is completed in the missionary command "Go therefore and make disciples of all nations" (Mt 28:19) and corresponds to the public nature of Christ's own teaching: "I have spoken openly to the world; I have always taught in synagogues and in the temple, where all Jews come together; I have said nothing secretly" (Jn 18:20; cf. Mk 14:49). On the other hand there is the saying of Christ which became the basis of the secret discipline of the early Christians: "Do not give dogs what is holy; and do not throw your pearls before swine, lest they trample them under foot and turn to attack you" (Mt 7:6). This is in accord with a certain reserve in Christ's teaching: "To you has been given the secret of the kingdom of God, but for those outside everything is in parables" (Mk 4:11).

---

[9] For the Christian, every man is ultimately a "brother", either as the "other brother" or as he with whom we are joined together in the unity of the "one brother". Apart from the primarily christological basis of this double brotherhood, the common fatherhood of God, of course, still stands in the background.

The problem hereby posed need not be pursued here in detail. The main point is that it is the role of the Church to speak to the world the word of God given in Christ, to witness before the world to the public saving work of God so that everyone can hear it. At the same time, however, she must perform this task with a holy discretion. She must not try to catch men with the word unawares, as it were, without their knowing it. She has no right to draw the word out of a hat, like a conjuror. And she must recognize that there are places where the word would be wasted, thrown away, if it were spoken. These considerations are important for the question of Church propaganda, as for example in religious broadcasting on radio and television.[10] He best disseminates the word who does not squander it (for what is too cheap or too easy is reckoned of little value) but proclaims it.

The second obligation of the Christian toward the non-Christian is agape. This takes two forms: first, the relations of Christians among one another ought to have an attractive and exemplary force, constituting an effective active mission. They should make Christians a "lamp on a stand" (Mk 4:21), a "city set on a hill" (Mt 5:14). "In the midst of a crooked and perverse generation" Christians are to "shine as lights in the world" (Phil 2:15). But all that is not enough. For these words of the Lord are meant for Christians too: "And

[10] For the discussion that arose some years ago on the theme of the Mass on television, see the full survey of the literature in *HK*, VII (1952–1953): 518–20, with references to the positions of Volk, Pieper, and Guardini who were opposed to it as, for other reasons, was K. Rahner, "The Mass and Television", *Mission and Grace,* I (London, 1963), 255–75.

if you salute only your brethren, what more are you doing than others? Do not even the Gentiles do the same?" (Mt 5:47). Christians can never, and must never, be satisfied with saluting and loving their brothers, that is, their fellow believers; they must follow the Lord who performed his work of love for those who neither knew nor loved him (see Rom 5:6), directing their love to all those who need them, without asking for thanks or a response. Everyone who needs their help is, by virtue of that, and independently of his own belief, a brother of Christ—in fact, a manifestation of the Lord himself (Mt 25:31–46). A true parousia of Christ takes place wherever a man recognizes and affirms the claim on his love that comes from a fellow man in need.

The last and highest mission of the Christian in relation to nonbelievers is to suffer for them and in their place as the Master did. At the end of his life, only a few days before his Passion, Christ described his life's mission in these words: "The Son of Man came not to be served but to serve, and to give his love as a ransom for many" (Mk 10:45). These words express not only the basic law of Christ's own life, but the basic law of all Christian discipleship. The disciples of Christ will always be "few", as the Lord said, and as such stand before the mass, the "many", as Jesus, the one, stands before the many (that is, the whole of mankind). "For the gate is narrow, and the way is hard that leads to life, and those who find it are few" (Mt 7:14; cf. v. 13: the "many" are those who go by the easy way to destruction). "The laborers are few" (Mt 9:37); "Few are chosen" (Mt 22:14, in contrast to the "many" called); "Fear not, little flock" (Lk 12:32); "Behold, I send you out as sheep in the midst of wolves"

(Mt 10:16). The disciples of Jesus are few, but as Jesus himself was one "for the many", so it will always be their mission to be not against but "for the many". When all other ways fail, there will always remain the royal way of vicarious suffering by the side of the Lord. It is in her defeat that the Church constantly achieves her highest victory and stands nearest to Christ. It is when she is called to suffer for others that she achieves her highest mission: the exchange of fate with the wayward brother and thus his secret restoration to full sonship and full brotherhood. Seen in this way, the relationship between the "few" and the "many" reveals the true measure of the Church's catholicity. In external numbers it will never be fully "catholic" (that is, all-embracing), but will always remain a small flock— smaller even than statistics suggest, statistics which lie when they call many "brothers" who are in fact merely *pseudadelphoi,* Christians by name only. In her suffering and love, however, she will always stand for the "many", for all. In her love and her suffering she surmounts all frontiers and is truly "catholic".

POSTSCRIPT

This discussion of the problem of Christian brotherhood has endeavored to apply what the New Testament says to the world today, even when what it says seems unexpected, even alien, to us. As I followed up the references, sometimes with surprise, in my mind there arose the question of the "separated brethren", the popular designation of Christians of differing confessions who thus express, across the gulf of their separation, their common adherence in faith to Jesus Christ, their brother. Must this formula be discarded because the New Testament restricts brotherhood, in the narrower sense, to those who share the one table, united through their common communion, which cannot exist among separated Christians? But then, what is the relation of these Christians to one another? Is the non-Catholic Christian, for a Catholic, the "other" brother only in the sense in which an unbaptized person is? Or does the community of baptism and the confession of the one Lord not, in fact, impart to him a greater share of fellowship? It is not easy to answer such questions, especially as they have seldom been asked in a sufficiently radical way, for fear of touching wounds that are still open. And yet it is necessary to ask this, just as truth is necessary for love.

The difficulty in the way of giving an answer is a profound one. Ultimately it is due to the fact that there is no appropriate category in Catholic thought for the phenomenon of Protestantism today (one could say the same of the relationship to the separated churches of the East). It is obvious that the old category of "heresy" is no longer of any value. Heresy, for Scripture and the early Church, includes the idea of a personal decision against the unity of the Church, and heresy's characteristic is *pertinacia,* the obstinacy of him who persists in his own private way. This, however, cannot be regarded as an appropriate description of the spiritual situation of the Protestant Christian. In the course of a now centuries-old history, Protestantism has made an important contribution to the realization of Christian faith, fulfilling a positive function in the development of the Christian message and, above all, often giving rise to a sincere and profound faith in the individual non-Catholic Christian, whose separation from the Catholic affirmation has nothing to do with the *pertinacia* characteristic of heresy. Perhaps we may here invert a saying of Saint Augustine's: that an old schism becomes a heresy. The very passage of time alters the character of a division, so that an old division is something essentially different from a new one. Something that was once rightly condemned as heresy cannot later simply become true, but it can gradually develop its own positive ecclesial nature, with which the individual is presented as his church and in which he lives as a believer, not as a heretic. This organization of one group, however, ultimately has an effect on the whole. The conclusion is inescapable, then: Protestantism today is something different from heresy in the traditional sense, a phenomenon whose true theological place has not yet been determined. And here resides the whole difficulty of the question we have asked. A phenomenon of this kind simply does not arise anywhere in the New Testament or in the Fathers; hence we have no direct guidance in them as to how we are to regard the separated Christians of today. Rather

we must try to think our way forward here in the spirit
of the New Testament and to apply this spirit to all
the things that did not exist then but are in our world
today. Such an attempt, which can be only barely outlined here and would need a lot of detailed preliminary
study, would have to start from the recognition that
in the mutual relationship of separated Christians there
are two levels that must be carefully distinguished: the
dogmatic one and the concrete moral one. The answer
differs according to the level about which we are speaking.

a. The dogmatic position is that the objective presentation of the vicarious saving act of Jesus Christ can be
performed by the one Church only, that is (according
to Catholic belief), the Catholic Church which is gathered around the successor of Peter. We come here to
the basic ecclesiological category (whose importance is
only now beginning to be recognized) of *re-praesentatio*.
Just as it is the essential nature of the sacraments to
show forth by signs the hidden mystery of God, to
proclaim publicly in the visible world the share of God
in the drama of history, to witness to the invisible deity
in the world of the visible, so it is with the great total
sacrament that is the Church herself: she is the sign of
God in the world, and her task is the visible and public
witness to the divine saving will before the face of history. Although she serves the realizing of grace, she
cannot simply be identified with grace. There is a difference between the symbolic presentation of the new order
of grace before the world and the presence or absence
of grace in a man's soul, which leads us into the hidden
secrets of the human heart which no one but God can
know. There is grace outside the sacraments and outside

the visible Church: the dialogue of God with man is conducted by him in total freedom; however, there is not some indeterminate number of churches or sacraments, but only the one sign of God through which he shows his mystery to the world. Once we see that the nature of the Church's existence is *re-praesentatio*—the public presentation of the saving reality of God—then it is obvious that there can be only one such valid sign. That does not mean that only Catholics make a positive contribution to the realizing of salvation, that only Catholics represent with Christ, while all others are merely represented and thus are only the negative shadow of Catholics. There is, rather, among individuals a great and interwoven pattern: what happens in the invisible order of grace is known ultimately to God alone who calls everyone by name, a name which he alone knows who receives it (cf. Rev 2:17). It is the objective presentation of this vicarious work of Christ that it is reserved for the one Church that, because of this continuation of the saving act of the Lord, can alone be called the "true" Church.

b. If we move now from the level of dogma to that of concrete human relationships, we can see from what we have said that the immediate brotherly community is made up of the communicants. Hence all those who are separated from the communion, in this case Protestants, do not belong to it. They have their own brotherhood, their own community. This is the nature of the divisions in the Church; some are no longer in communion with others, and thus sharing in the brotherhood of the Church (which was to be only one, according to the will of the Lord) is made impossible. And so, if the immediate narrow fraternal community is made up only of the believers of the one Church, we can ask at least that the two communities—Catholic and Protestant—regard each other as "sisters in the Lord". This is an idea which goes beyond Scripture and the Fathers (here, as we have seen, there is only the sisterliness of the Catholic communities), but which seems justified by the new situation of separated Christians. Both communities, as bearers of faith in an unbelieving world, can and should regard themselves as sisters, and individual Christians on both sides are "brothers" to each other in a far more fundamental sense than are non-Christians. Admittedly, this brotherhood between Catholics and Protestants includes the fact that both belong to a different fraternal community—includes, too, the separation, and the pain of this separation, and thus presents a constant challenge to overcome it. Indeed, it is important not to ignore the element of separation which is inevitably part of this brotherhood and gives it its particular quality: to ignore it is ultimately to become reconciled to it, and that is just what we must not do. "Separated brethren", which has become such a glib phrase, can thus acquire an exact and valuable meaning. It expresses the unity that remains as well as the tragedy of division. Thus the phrase should be a comfort, and also a spur—a spur that does not let us rest until there is "one flock, one shepherd" (Jn 10:16).

Abbreviations

Cath	*Catholica*
CCSL	*Corpus Christianorum Series Latina*
CSEL	*Corpus Scriptorum Ecclesiasticorum Latinorum*
DACL	*Dictionnaire d'archéologie chrétienne et de liturgie*
HK	*Herderkorrespondenz*
LTK	*Lexikon für Theologie und Kirche*
MTZ	*Münchener theologische Zeitschrift*
PW-*RKA*	Pauly and Wissowa, *Realenzyklopadie der klassichen Altertumswissenschaften*
RAC	*Reallexikon für Antike und Christentum*
RGG	*Religion in Geschichte und Gegenwart*
SB-*KNT*	Strack and Billerbeck, *Kommentar zum neuen Testament aus Talmud und Midrash*
TQ	*Theologische Quartalschift*
TWNT	*Theologisches Wörterbuch zum neuen Testament*, ed. V. G. Kittel